Tunny

The rise and fall
of Britain's biggest fish

Tunny

The rise and fall
of Britain's biggest fish

Chris Berry

MEDLAR PRESS

Published by The Medlar Press Limited,
The Grange, Ellesmere, Shropshire SY12 9DE
www.medlarpress.com

ISBN 978-1-907110-03-0

Text © Chris Berry, 2010
Design © The Medlar Press, 2010
Reprinted 2020

The author and publisher would like to thank all those who
have given permission for copyright material to be reproduced
in this book. If any have been inadvertently overlooked they
will be pleased to make the necessary arrangements.

Designed and typeset in 12 on 13 point Garamond Roman.
Produced in England by The Medlar Press Limited, Ellesmere, England.

[4]

Contents

Author's Note

Even a small book such as this requires a number of kind people, without whom it would never see the light of day. Jon and Rose Ward-Allen have been particularly patient, while many others have contributed their time, knowledge and wisdom. My grateful thanks go to Chris Quinn, Phil Arnott, Georgina Ingham, Sarah Birtles, Tim Birtles, Vincent Hedley-Lewis, Bill Pashby, Faith Young, Robert Fletcher Dunn, David Holdsworth, David Buchanan, and the people of Yorkshire's East Coast, past and present.

Last but not least, thanks must go to my brother Jon, who would have written this book had he not been busy with other tales, and my cousin Ricky, who first showed me what fun chasing fish could be.

For my son Ed,
who makes every fishing trip an adventure.

Preface

It were easy in them days . . .

In the North Sea, shortly before dawn, three boats are at work. The first is a huge herring trawler, its deck lights piercing the crepuscular gloom. Nearby, in its wake, sits a wooden coble, some forty feet long. On a rope behind the coble is the third craft, a simple rowing boat. It looks incongruous, too tiny to be out here, some ten miles from land, and as yet nobody has clambered aboard. But that is about to change.

Suddenly, for a brief, electrifying moment, the dorsal fin of an enormous fish cuts the surface. On the coble, there is a flurry of activity. A young boy of perhaps ten years of age picks up a handful of herrings and tosses them into the black waves. Instantly, the water boils. Behind the boy a stout gentleman straps on a leather harness and steps carefully into the rowing boat, carrying a short, brutish-looking fishing rod. His oarsman, a weathered-looking man of indeterminate age, steels himself for what he knows is about to happen.

More herrings are thrown overboard and seized by the unseen predator. On the rowing boat a 6-inch hook is carefully baited, then lowered overboard. For long moments, nothing happens. The thirty second wait feels like an eternity, but finally, incredibly, a fish takes. One of the men shouts, nobody is sure who, and the angler braces his feet and sets the hook. The result is explosive. A huge tunny sets off in a blistering, heart-stopping run, somehow avoiding both the keel of the nearby coble and the cod end of the trawler's net. For two, maybe three hundred yards it runs unchecked, before the angler gradually applies the brake, tentatively at first, then more confidently. Eventually, the run is stopped. An impasse of sorts is reached, and the unseen tunny is steadily towing the rowing boat against the tide.

The next forty minutes are not spectacular. The fish does not jump, the angler makes little attempt at gaining line and the battle, to the observer at least, is a dour war of attrition. By the end the fish is barely alive, many fathoms down, and the angler struggles to raise it to the surface, mere inches at a time. And then it appears, a huge tunny some eight feet in length and well over six hundred pounds in weight, utterly defeated but not quite dead, still a magnificent creature of subtle blues, yellows and greens. Only when it is gaffed and dragged on to the coble does it finally lose its lustre. It is a perfect if average-sized example of the bluefin tuna, or tunny, Britain's biggest ever fish.

* * *

Over fifty years later, a stiff breeze chills the cluster of anglers huddled on the Vincent Pier as the *Regal Lady* nudges its way out of the Old Harbour, past the lighthouse and out into the North Sea. In the wheelhouse is Bill Pashby, half a century after he helped land the last tunny caught off Scarborough. Deftly avoiding the craft of less seasoned skippers, memories of his youth, and the halcyon days of British big game fishing, come flooding back.

Between 1930 and 1954, each August and September, Scarborough was transformed by tunny fishing. Giant bluefin tuna, often averaging 600lb in weight, would appear offshore and anglers would battle them from rowing boats towed to the fishing grounds by cobles, keel boats and luxury yachts. The anglers were a heady mix of aristocrats, film stars, industrialists and high ranking military types, but the real heroes were Scarborough's local fishermen. Bill Pashby, like his father before him, was at the centre of it all.

"It were easy in them days," he smiles. "Around the tenth of August the herring would come in. The ships would be six to ten miles off, Dutch, Russian, German, and Scotch, hundreds of them. At night the sea was lit up like a town. You'd just go to the first ship with a crate of beer, and ask whether they'd seen any tunny fish."

For the schoolboy son of a Scarborough fishing family, chasing giant 'tunny fish' with the rich sports that flocked to the seaside town was an annual adventure. "To us it were a holiday. I was excited. Bear in mind there were whales out there too. We were long-lining for dogfish out of Grimsby, but we'd come back when the tunny were in. Just imagine it, no wind, and the water crystal clear, it was marvellous. And if the weather was bad, we still got paid!"

As a young boy, Bill was spared the task of rowing a small boat after a hooked tunny. That was men's work. It was Bill's job to get the tunny feeding in the first place, usually as the trawlers and drifters hauled their nets. "I was on the big boat, my dad's keel boat *Courage*, chucking herring over the side when the nets came up."

Clearly, the tactic worked. The Pashbys' most regular client, Mr H. E. Weatherley of Teddington, was by far the most prolific member of the British Tunny Club in its final days. But even he had his limit. On 24th August, 1950, fishing from *Courage*, he landed a staggering quartet - tunny of 589, 545, 743 and 714lb. "He had four fish before breakfast," recalls Bill, "and he came alongside. He was tired out by then. I was in the big boat and said 'Come on Mr Weatherley, they're still around us.' He just looked at me and said 'Impetuous youth!'"

Times have changed. Most of the men and women who chased tunny off Scarborough have long gone, as have the trawlers, drifters and huge shoals of herring that brought nomadic tunny to the North Yorkshire coast. Rumours of the tunny's return still surface occasionally, but until they do, Scarborough, and Bill Pashby, can always remember the glory days of British monster hunting . . .

1

Early Days
1914 - 1932

Imagine a quarter of a ton of solid muscle pulling at you!
It's wonderful. Sometimes they tow the boat for miles.

Fishermen knew all about the tunny long before anyone managed to land one on rod and line. The word 'tunny' first appeared in English literature in the 1350s, but bluefin tuna, as they are known outside British waters, have been harvested for at least two millennia. In the late nineteenth century, however, as big game fishing became increasingly popular, it was inevitable that some brave soul would want to try and outwit a tunny through sporting means. To do so, they would need tackle capable of withstanding a 500-yard run from a fish weighing well in excess of a quarter of a ton. Until the late nineteenth and early twentieth century, such tackle simply didn't exist.

As with much of tunny fishing history, the capture of the first fish is a murky affair. According to David Carl Forbes, writing in 1972, 'sport fishing for tunny started in the 1870s, out of Liverpool, Nova Scotia, and the first rod-caught fish is credited to a schoolteacher named Thomas Patillo. He eventually returned to port with a 600lb tunny, and the acclaim of the populace.' Patillo's 1871 capture certainly took place, and on home-made tackle too, but it was far from unassisted. At one point, he had to enlist help to get his fish cut free from nets in which it was tangled, thus breaking one of the central laws which would later define sport fishing for tuna.

The more common view is that tunny fishing, by proper sporting means at least, started much later. The pioneer was none other than Lorenzo Mitchell-Henry, a name synonymous with the birth of Scarborough's tunny years, and one we will return to again and again in this tale.

Mitchell-Henry was certainly the driving force behind much of the tackle which brought giant tunny within reach of mere mortals. An industrialist by trade and innovator by nature, he put his considerable talents towards creating tackle capable of dealing with the rigours of tunny fishing. As he wrote in 1934, with a characteristic lack of false modesty, 'In the design and construction of tackle for this great fish, I played a lone hand as far back as 1908.'

'It is nearly 30 years since I first heard of the giant Atlantic tunny off Cape Breton, Nova Scotia,' recalled Mitchell-Henry in 1934. 'I at once recognised that the tackle then existing would be totally inadequate with which to attempt the capture on rod and line of one of these mighty fish.'

Mitchell-Henry, however, was not a man to be beaten by such obstacles, and his combination of engineering knowledge and big fish experience was ideal for the task. What some had seen as insurmountable difficulties, he saw as a challenge: 'As I had been actively interested in big game fishing for some 20 years before that date, I was thoroughly familiar with the sport as then practised in America. My imagination was immediately fired by the possibilities . . . I began at once to plan a campaign and to determine the methods and tackle which would be required to capture a fish of so great a speed, size and weight.'

In 1914, Mitchell-Henry travelled to Port Medway, Nova Scotia, with his new tunny tackle. There he met with Captain

Mitchell-Henry's first tunny.

The final act as the tunny comes aboard.

Contemplating the first tunny.

Mitchell-Henry with his first tunny.

Laurie Mitchell, who ran a small fisherman's lodge with two motorboats and a brace of skiffs. His host's stories, according to Mitchell-Henry, were encouraging on the one hand, terrifying on the other: 'The tale he unfolded to me of his experiences and those of his guests in combat with the giant tunny were astounding, for of seventy-nine fish which they had hooked in the past eight years, not one of them had been landed.'

Clearly Mitchell-Henry had every chance of hooking his quarry, but would his new tackle be up to the job? 'The test,' he said, 'was not long in coming, for on the first day out I succeeded in landing a fish of 520lb after a severe fight of over four hours. This was the first tunny ever caught on rod and line unaided, in the open sea off Nova Scotia.'

The Mitchell-Henry reel.

The battle had been an epic one. Mitchell-Henry fought his fish in a worsening sea, and photographs show waves threatening to swamp his small boat as the fish was brought to the gaff. At the end he described himself as 'absolutely all in', but it was obviously worth the effort. The tunny won Mitchell-Henry the prestigious Forest and Stream Trophy, which remained one of his most treasured possessions.

Nor did the action end there. In subsequent days more tunny were hooked, although again and again they were lost as various bits of tackle gave way. Ten fish were lost through breakages of highly-tempered hooks, although on his last day, Mitchell-Henry landed a second fish of 480lb. As a fitting epithet, Captain Mitchell also hooked a tunny, just as his guest headed for shore to catch the train home. Using spare tackle left behind by Mitchell-Henry, he eventually landed a fish of 710lb, a new world record and justifiable reward for eight years of heroic failure.

* * *

With the outbreak of the Great War, tunny fishing ceased, but Mitchell-Henry hadn't given up on tunny by any means. In 1926 he developed an improved reel and harness, although it was not until the following year that he was able to travel to Norway to use them in anger. Alas, he suffered a rare failure, finding rough seas and no signs of tunny, but in 1928 he shifted his focus to Denmark, where he managed to land tunny up to 523lb. Other anglers soon heard about Mitchell-Henry's endeavours, 'and a merry time we had fighting our battles over again and comparing and testing tackle . . . my equipment was far in advance of that being commonly used.'

In 1929 eight tunny were landed in the Kattegat, an arm of the North Sea between Sweden and Denmark. Mitchell-Henry managed only one, despite his superior tackle, while William Ramsay and F. B. Hannam each managed a leash. The biggest weighed 514lb and featured, belatedly, in the *Fishing Gazette* on 1st March, 1930.

In these early days, tunny fishing was confined to a small, tight-knit community. Competitiveness and internecine squabbling were yet to surface, with Mitchell-Henry acting as the sport's kindly father figure. F. B. Hannam, writing in the *British Sea Anglers' Society's Quarterly*, strikes an almost hagiographic tone: 'I would like to start straight away by saying that no one I have ever met could possibly have been more cheery, more entertaining, more thoughtful of my comfort, more willing to do more than his share of the heavy work, more full of fun at the end of a physically tiring day - and we had many of them - than Mr Mitchell-Henry proved on this holiday. He was always calm, unruffled, resourceful, quick of thought and quicker of action, possessing more strength and vitality than many men half our age.'

On one occasion, travelling to Copenhagen with Mitchell-Henry, a weary Hannam had been loudly longing for a hot bath. Arriving at the hotel, Mitchell-Henry had darted inside first, arranging for a room key and steaming bath to be ready

Mitchell-Henry fighting a tunny off Denmark in 1928.

upon his friend's arrival. It was only when a refreshed Hannam returned to the hotel lobby that he discovered Mitchell-Henry had given him the last remaining room, and 'would probably have to sleep out'. These small acts of kindness typified their holiday and it is little wonder that Hannam remained one of Mitchell-Henry's staunchest supporters.

During his Scandinavian adventures, with typical thoroughness, Mitchell-Henry had kept in touch with the commercial drifters and trawlers working the North Sea, and rumours were slowly emerging of tunny off Scarborough. Indeed, The *Fishing Gazette* had published a letter in September 1926 from a correspondent calling himself A.D.M., who had managed to land one from an undisclosed area of the North Sea. Few details were given, but it was obviously a less than sporting capture: 'We had no rod and line worthy of the name, but with very crude weapons we managed to hook and land a tunny . . . We had no means of finding the exact weight, but its length was 7 foot 10 inches and its girth 5 foot 8 inches.'

The editor of *The Field* used the Tuna Club of America's formula to calculate a weight of nearly 550lb, although he felt this far too heavy for a British fish and settled on a more conservative estimate of 400-450lb. Given what was to happen in a few short years, his first figure may have been closer to the mark.

A Scarborough fisherman, Billy Watkinson, had seen plenty of tunny in the Mediterranean during his wartime naval service, and suggested that the strange predators talked about by local herring boats were the same fish. Local naturalist W. J. Clarke, better known as 'Old Fuzzy', agreed with him. Their views reached not just Mitchell-Henry but Colonel R. F. Stapleton-Cotton, who in 1929, on his first attempt, connected with two huge fish only to lose them when the hooks pulled out. Mitchell-Henry's own first visit was too late in the season, and he spent a highly unpleasant night in the cramped wheelhouse of a trawler in a heavy gale. Unsurprisingly, he didn't catch, but 1930 would see Mitchell-Henry back in Scarborough in good time for any tunny that might appear.

Tunny fever had begun, albeit in a low-key way. A local businessman had offered 50 shillings for a tunny and a Yarmouth drifter called *Ascendant* landed one of 560lb. Now it was just up to the sport fisherman to repeat the same feat.

The year1930, some might say, was the one that changed Scarborough completely. Hitherto it had been a picturesque and genteel seaside resort where, in 1626, Mrs Elizabeth Farrow is said to have invented the seaside holiday. Her discovery of an effervescent spring, which she called a 'most Sovereign remedy against Hypondriack, Melancholly and Windiness', led to Scarborough becoming the world's first beach resort. By the early twentieth century it was a town best summed up by Tom Laughton, hotelier, tunny fisherman and brother of actor Charles, in his book *Pavilions by the Sea*: 'Scarborough was a very class conscious town. "The best people" resided on the South Cliff, tradesmen and shopkeepers lived and worked in the centre, the lodgings and boarding houses were mostly on the North Side. On the front the divisions were marked by the Spa, the exclusive resort of the prosperous and respectable with a sprinkling of the aristocracy.'

Scarborough would soon be even more illustrious as it became the epicentre of big game angling, attracting fishermen from all over the world. In the words of Fred Taylor, author of *Tunny Fishing for Beginners* (1934), 'The real start of big-game angling in British waters came in 1930, when on 27th August Mr Mitchell-Henry made history by landing the first fish ever caught here on rod and line.'

Mitchell-Henry made only brief reference to this fish in his own book, no doubt because he had by now taken several tunny overseas, but it created a stir in the British weekly press. Perhaps fittingly, it was 'Old Fuzzy' Clarke who broke the news, in two letters published in the *Fishing Gazette* on 6th September of that year. In the first, written while the fish was still to be hauled ashore, he explained that 'I was unable to get a word with Mr Mitchell-Henry, but from statements made by members of his crew I gather that the fish was caught some 60 miles from Scarborough, and that it took about two hours to bring to the gaff. Mr Mitchell-Henry estimates the weight at about 400lb.'

This was a very conservative estimate. Clarke's second letter recorded that Britain's first rod-caught tunny 'measures 8ft 6 in. in total length, 5ft 4in. in girth, and weighs 560lb'. Such conspicuous success naturally attracted other anglers to Scarborough, and 1930 eventually saw five tunny landed. It also saw the start of Hardy's public association with the tunny fraternity. A full page advert on 13th September showed Colonel Stapleton-Cotton with a fish of 630lb, proudly adding that it had been caught on a Hardy No. 5 Salt Water rod and 9-inch Fortuna Big Game Sea Fish Reel. Two weeks later the same fish was again featured, this time alongside a 392lb specimen caught by the company's Scarborough agent, Harold J. Hardy, and the new 'British record' of 735lb, caught by Fred Taylor.

Hardy's fish was the only one landed of eight that he hooked, and was beaten after a fight of an hour and forty minutes. In the first of many such claims, he tried to 'correct any misapprehension that may have arisen as to the cost of tackle, etc. What I used, including gaff and necessary spares, can be bought for about £50.'

In October Hardy was again in the *Fishing Gazette*, explaining that while he had yet to catch another, the North Sea was still alive with tunny chasing the herring fleet. 'Two large shoals of tunny arrived,' he wrote. 'The tunny behaved just like a shoal of mackerel, and came up literally in dozens at a time. It was a magnificent sight. Many of them were much larger than I have seen before, and must have weighed in excess of 1,000lb. At a guess their numbers must have been well over three figures.'

Despite their abundance, Taylor's 735lb fish remained the biggest capture of Scarborough's first tunny season. It was a sure sign, though, that the East Coast could produce giants to rival those of Nova Scotia.

* * *

After the 1930 season, hopes were high for 1931. With more anglers, improving tackle and a greater shared knowledge of the tunny's habits, expectations were soaring and Scarborough buzzed with anticipation from midsummer onwards. On 22nd August, again in the *Fishing Gazette*, 'Old Fuzzy' Clarke wrote that 'Many reports of tunnies in abundance are being received from the fishing boats. The fish are coming closer inshore, two boats having seen shoals only seven miles out. A single fish was seen in the Bay only one mile from land. The sea is still too rough for anglers to go in search of them.'

In the same issue, Colonel Stapleton-Cotton explained to readers just how easy this new business of tunny fishing was. 'The whole thing is so simple,' he declared, 'and so certain that it may be worthwhile your publishing this letter. Two things you must have, fine weather and tuna within reasonable distance of the shore. Given those factors it is a practical certainty of hooking fish provided you get to the drifters before dawn . . . I am open to bet a sovereign he will hook fish every day he goes out.'

Such confidence was misplaced, and Fred Taylor sums up 1931 better than anyone. 'Fate dealt a cruel blow,' he laments. 'Over my own experiences of that season, and that of many other anglers as well, it would be best to draw a veil. During the whole period, only one fish was landed - again it was by Mr Mitchell-Henry, and again it weighed 560lb. I never even saw a fin.'

News of Mitchell-Henry's fish was broadcast by the BBC, who announced that it was 9 foot long and took six hours to land. 'We congratulate Mr Mitchell-Henry on his feat,' added the *Fishing Gazette*, remarking that 'playing a fish of 560lb for six hours would be a real test of endurance for a young man, and Mr Mitchell-Henry is 64.'

Taylor struck a philosophical note about his own failure, claiming 'It is good for one to go through trials and tribulations, like we did then; it gives one a deeper appreciation of sport and some of its difficulties.' More prosaically, though, he added that 'Tunny fishing is undoubtedly a fair weather sport. The weather in 1931 was atrocious.'

Mitchell-Henry agreed: 'The season of 1931 proved to be a wretched one. Gale succeeded gale all through the summer, and owing to the low temperature, the fish kept a long way off shore. That year a large number of sportsmen were out fishing, and one lady had the hard luck to lose a good fish through the breaking of a faulty line, which was most disappointing to her, and indeed to all of us; we were unanimous in wishing her better luck next time.'

F. B. Hannam best summed up the frustrations of tunny fishing in 1931, or rather not fishing, due to poor weather, in the

BSAS Quarterly. 'I am afraid that cursing seemed to be appropriate,' he wrote. 'The Scarborough weather must have had a deteriorating effect on my character . . . we started at 8.30 in a rough sea, as there was a possibility of a calmer afternoon. We went some 21 miles E.N.E., saw nothing, heard nothing, and met two other searchers who also saw nothing. The wind freshened instead of dropping, so we went home in the usual state of annoyance.'

There were, however, a few light-hearted moments. Hannam was ruefully pleased when, on overhearing hardy local fishermen discussing the tunny anglers' battles with the weather, one of them remarked, "It's marvellous how these men stick it." On another occasion he saw a small sunfish sold for two shillings at the pier, but when the auctioneer spotted Hannam he declared that it was worth far more than a tunny and held a mock sale, aided and abetted by local buyers, 'selling' it for £11 to the astonishment of a crowd who were oblivious to the joke. It was another sign of the acceptance tunny anglers were gaining in Scarborough. Now all they needed was some luck.

* * *

In 1932, they got it. The North Sea was alive with tunny, not to mention tunny anglers, and that year it was generally the anglers who prevailed. 'During those few weeks England made angling history,' wrote Fred Taylor. 'Twenty-one fish were landed, with an *average* weight of slightly under 600lb. Several were over 700lb and Colonel E. T. Peel had the proud distinction of landing a magnificent specimen of 798lb which beat the previous world's record by 40lb. In addition, Mrs Sparrow showed what ladies could do, and landed a beautiful fish of 469lb. A splendid performance.'

No tunny season would be complete without its failures, of course, and one in particular stood out. Harold J. Hardy reported fishing with Mr G. Heneage, who lost three fish on 10th August. The first two were fleeting encounters, with the hooks barely penetrating, but the last was nothing short of a disaster. 'The third he fought for seven hours and ten minutes,' wrote Hardy, 'when we managed to get it alongside to gaff. Perhaps we were a bit too quick and the stroke missed. The man holding the trace let go when the gaffing stroke was made, and the whole weight came suddenly on the line. The fish made a dying flurry and broke the line near the trace . . . the largest tunny I have so far seen. A tragedy as we practically had him safe. He was undoubtedly a world record fish.' Heneage's tunny had towed him over seventeen miles during the battle and, according to Old Fuzzy Clarke, was approximately sixteen feet long and weighed in excess of 1,000lb.

Hardy also had his share of bad luck. Sixteen days after Heneage's lost leviathan, his companion hooked and lost eight fish in succession. F. B. Hannam, whose own season was frequently blighted by porbeagle sharks chasing the tunny away, was keen to point out that these losses were due not to poor angling but to Hardy's experimental nature. Rather than fish from the conventional rowing boat, pulled by a tender, he was trying out a motorised coble in an effort to reduce the cost of tunny fishing by 30 shillings a day. Quite what the burgeoning boat hire business thought of this is uncertain, although Hannam offered a clue in the *BSAS Quarterly*: 'On arrival at Scarborough I saw a lot of men who I had met in previous years, and they all started to tell me, gloatingly, how many fish Mr Hardy had hooked and lost. I am afraid I did not increase my popularity by the manner in which I shut them up.'

Another angler to rue his luck was Sir Digby Warren, who in 1932 was still to land his first tunny despite two years of trying. When he finally hooked his monster it smashed his rod, but Warren held on for four hours, slowly gaining ground on the fish, before it broke free. A poem oft-quoted by Hannam may have sprung to mind:

Pray God that if a fish is lost
I do not break my rod in half;
And that, no matter what the cost,
I do not curse but still can laugh.

Elsewhere, others were faring rather better. On the same day that Hardy lost eight, Colonel Peel managed a tunny of 714lb, despite breaking his rod during the fight, while the following day Mr B. Clyde Smith battled a 721lb fish for over six hours, getting towed twenty-five miles in the process. Colonel Peel, who seemed to be getting more tunny than most, was keen to praise the role of the herring fishermen. 'What they toil at, we play at,' he said, 'but they give us all the information and hospitality they can, and are keen to help. They all hail us when there are fish. They are just as keen to get us a big fish even if they themselves have got nothing on board after a night's work.' To show his gratitude, Colonel Peel sold two of his tunny that week for £13, and donated the proceeds to a fund for repairing the fishermen's damaged nets.

Mitchell-Henry, of course, enjoyed another successful year, despite shifting his base to Whitby. For the third season in a row he took the first tunny, in this case a fish of 700lb, with three more following, including another 700-pounder. He may, however, have beaten the record, had it not been for an unfortunate contretemps with another vessel: 'I had the disappointment of having my line severed by a trawler crossing it when engaged in a thrilling fight with the biggest fish I have ever had hold of. I was well set for a world's record. It was unfortunate to lose so fine a chance this way.'

* * *

Thus ended the sport's age of innocence, a time when tunny fishing was the preserve of a small band of pioneering anglers. Until 1932 it had been conducted under the auspices of the

British Sea Anglers' Society, who offered two classes of certificate for tunny caught: rowing-boat and motor-boat certificates. After the successes of 1932, however, tunny fishing was a rapidly growing phenomenon, with very different demands to conventional sea angling. The rules initially drawn up by the BSAS were already outdated and there was clearly a need for a specialist organising body that could define a new set of sporting ethics.

In October 1932, with the tunny season over for the year, changes were afoot. The *Fishing Gazette*, by now the unofficial weekly journal of the tunny fraternity, had argued for a new organisation, but Arthur Bell, Honorary Secretary of the BSAS, was quick to correct them. 'I think it should be pointed out that a Tunny Club already exists within the British Sea Anglers' Society. The Society was entirely responsible for the discovery and introduction of British tunny fishing, and up to this year every fish caught was taken by a member. I respectfully suggest that if those considering the formation of a separate tunny club will get in touch with this society, much time and expense will be saved.'

BSAS (Big Game) declaration form.

Meetings were held during November and the British Tunny Club was soon established, albeit without the close affiliation that Arthur Bell had been seeking. By December of that year the new Joint Honorary Secretaries, Harold J. Hardy and Eric Cooper, were writing to *The Times* to announce the venture:

Sir, with the advent during the last few years of tunny fishing in the North Sea the need for a club to control the sport has become manifest. The club is now in being and is named the British Tunny Club. The club will draw up big-game fishing rules and place on record details of all fish caught and generally see that these are caught in a sporting manner. In the framing of these rules it is the sincere wish of the committee that all anglers with a knowledge of this sport will give their help, and, with this object in view may we ask big-game anglers to write to us with any suggestions they may care to put forward?

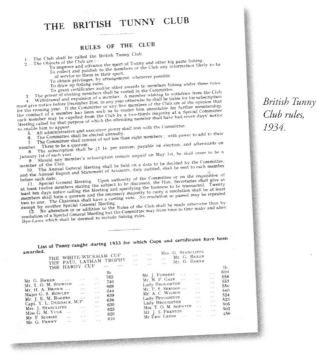

British Tunny Club rules, 1934.

Opposite: *A view of Scarborough and (inset) the Tunny Club headquarters in the early 1950s.*

Their letter struck a conciliatory note, but control of the sport had already caused tensions, with the new club and the BSAS potentially at odds. In the years that followed, Lorenzo Mitchell-Henry would seek to expose this rift, repeatedly and publicly calling for the British Tunny Club to disband and relinquish control to the BSAS. For now, though, there was a real sense of optimism and the British Tunny Club's momentum was too strong for even Mitchell-Henry. The new organisation soon established its headquarters at No. 1 Sandgate, in a building provided free by a Scarborough Council grateful for the money tunny anglers brought to the town. Following a grand opening by Mayor J. K. C. Pindar, they got to work. It was a time of great excitement, but even the more excitable members cannot have imagined the club would soon become such a remarkable part of angling's social history.

Engraving of a tunny from Pennant's British Zoology, *1776.*

2

Big Fish, Butlers and Bentleys

The tunny is not an easy fish...
it is as wary and artful as a bass.

In the history of British tunny fishing, one name looms large. Without Lorenzo Mitchell-Henry, the tunny fishing boom in Scarborough would arguably still have happened, but it would not have been as successful, as colourful or, in many ways, as controversial.

Mitchell-Henry, or 'M-H' as his friends called him, was born in his father's substantial Knightsbridge home in 1866, and followed his older brothers to Eton. After school he was commissioned into the Royal Monmouthshire Regiment Royal Engineers, an early forerunner of the Territorials, where he honed the shooting prowess he had shown from an early age. Thereafter he divided his time between Knightsbridge, from which he enjoyed all that society life had to offer, and Kyle-more Castle, a huge sporting estate in County Galway.

It was at the latter that he berthed his self-designed steam yacht, *Ida*, an early flirtation with life afloat, and installed a turbine plant to harness water running off the hill behind his castle. It was exactly the sort of innovative engineering which would typify his later fishing exploits.

Throughout his life, Mitchell-Henry loved anything new or

innovative. In the 1890s motoring became his latest fascination, and he was one of the first to make the 100-mile run from London to Brighton and back within a day. He also joined the Royal Automobile Club, from whose Pall Mall rooms he would later pen many of his letters to *The Field* and the *Fishing Gazette*.

Mitchell-Henry would invariably invent solutions for whatever problems he encountered. His aims were not commercial - he was already wealthy - and several of his designs made a lot of money when copied by others. Perhaps most famously, Mitchell-Henry was the first to place metal bridges on spectacles, either side of the nose, to make them more comfortable, but a more lucrative invention was the smokeless Henrite shotgun cartridge. Mitchell-Henry was an internationally renowned 'pigeon shot' - a live bird equivalent of clay pigeon shooting, long since banned in this country - and sales of his much-improved cartridge were brisk.

Mitchell-Henry, however, was not a man to stand still. Even the contrasting pleasures of London and Galway could not contain him and he soon made his way to the United States. It was here he turned down the chance to invest in the fledgling company of an ambitious young mechanic - the mechanic's name was Henry Ford - but he did at least meet and marry Marion, the beautiful daughter of a wealthy New York lawyer. They later settled in London, although Mitchell-Henry continued to travel as his interest in big game fishing grew.

Mitchell-Henry had been big game fishing for several years before he turned his attention to tunny. He did so with the thoroughness that he applied to everything in life, refusing to believe that certain things just could not be done, and in retrospect it is hardly surprising that he succeeded off Nova Scotia, when so many others had failed before.

It was on this trip, in 1914, using Mitchell-Henry's own tackle, that Captain Laurie Mitchell landed a 710lb fish which became the new world record. Ten years later his tunny was superseded by another of 758lb, but the circumstances of its capture were somewhat different, and not to Mitchell-Henry's taste. 'This was done from a fast, twin-engined motorboat,' he wrote in *Tunny Fishing at Home and Abroad*, '[and] I have always considered Captain Mitchell's fish as the record captured in a sporting manner.'

Noble sentiments, perhaps, for sport fishing in the 1930s had sensibilities sadly lacking in much twenty-first century angling, but it would not be the last time Mitchell-Henry publicly denounced a new record caught by somebody else.

Mitchell-Henry, by the early 1930s, was the pre-eminent figure in international tunny fishing. He was the first to catch a fish off Nova Scotia, the first to land one in Europe, off Norway, and, of course, he caught the first Scarborough tunny in 1930. He was, Fred Taylor noted, 'as everyone knows, the great pioneer of tunny fishing'. His achievements were not so much measured in numbers of fish, for others eventually caught more and arguably bigger tunny, but Mitchell-Henry was always there first.

His fish were also caught on tackle of his own design, developed and tested against tarpon, sharks and, on one memorable occasion, a motor car. Legend has it that when Mitchell-Henry finally built a rod and reel he considered sufficiently strong for a tunny, he attached a hook to the bumper of his Bentley and battled it as his butler tried to drive away. Alas, the results of his experiment were not recorded for posterity, but we do know that Mitchell-Henry set off for Nova Scotia shortly after.

In later years, his tackle testing took a more scientific, less decadent turn. In *Angler's Cavalcade* (1966), Eric Horsfall Turner recalls his first encounter with the sport's father figure. 'I thought I knew quite a bit about the game,' he wrote, 'then I joined Mitchell-Henry, or M-H as we usually call him, for lunch at the Royal Automobile Club, in Pall Mall. He was wearing a very worn Old Etonian tie, and after our short snack, he

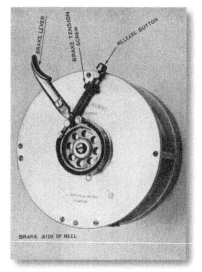

Detail of the Mitchell-Henry reel.

pulled out a massive Havana cigar. He waved aside the offer of gin and whisky as vile stuff . . . later we went to the large shed at the back of his small house in Ealing. It was fitted out as a first class workshop. His tackle experiments, inventions and equipment showed remarkable ingenuity. I even sat, strapped to a swivel seat, playing the equivalent of a 1000lb tunny against a complex mechanism of pulleys, springs and a heavy weight.'

'I reached the conclusion,' he concluded, 'that the run of tunny experts I had met were elementary performers by comparison.'

Mitchell-Henry would have expected no less. He was not, after all, given to false modesty, nor would he seek to play down the influence he had on tunny fishing. Most of his tackle innovations, for example, were eponymously named, from the Mitchell-Henry reel to the Mitchell-Henry Patented Line Guard, Mitchell-Henry Patent Spring Link, Mitchell-Henry Patented Hook, Mitchell-Henry Top Pulley, Mitchell-Henry Square Ended Stirrup, Mitchell-Henry Balance Handle, Mitchell-Henry Brace Harness and so on.

The archetypal British angler was rather more diffident, but then Mitchell-Henry was no archetype. A man before his time, and no doubt influenced by some of the rather more publicity-hungry elements of American big game fishing, he was determined to leave his mark, and his name, on the world. Given the branding of modern celebrity anglers, Mitchell-Henry's desire for fame seems tame some seventy years later, but at the time it was not the stuff of English piscators.

Tunny fishing would never have begun, however, had Mitchell-Henry not developed the tackle, at his own time and expense, capable of landing them. F. B. Hannam, who fished with him in Odden during the late Twenties, is in no doubt where the credit for all those tunny really belongs. 'It would be a comparatively simple thing to teach a child of twelve to drive a Rolls Royce from London to Brighton,' he wrote in 'Tussles with Tunnies' (*BSAS Quarterly*), 'but the credit for such an achievement surely should go to the designers and manufacturers of the car and also the teacher. Very little credit, if any, is due to the child. In the same way I should like to point out that, in fishing, very little praise should be given to the angler . . . the designers and makers of the rod, reel and rest of the outfit are the people to whom the credit should be attributed.' According to Hannam it was Mitchell-Henry, as both manufacturer and teacher in the sport's formative years, who deserved the lion's share of the acclaim.

Nor, to be fair, was Mitchell-Henry the most self-aggrandising big game angler of the time. Zane Grey, an American who carefully cultivated his own legend, far exceeded the Englishman in self-publicity. The two men were not friends, to put it mildly, and Mitchell-Henry devoted a full ten pages of his book to refuting some of Grey's accusations. Their spat, which also spilled over into the pages of the angling press, was a clash of cultures, personalities, ethics and, more than anything, egos.

In 1931, Grey had written what the *Fishing Gazette* termed an anti-British 'outburst' in an American magazine, *Outdoor Life*, regarding the ethics of big game, and specifically tunny fishing. The *Gazette* was not about to have British angling honour besmirched and gave a withering response: 'So far as we can see, Mr Grey has succeeded only in getting himself thoroughly disliked.'

The editor of *Outdoor Life* did not publish Mitchell-Henry's response, so the feud festered until Zane Grey wrote an article in *The Field*, once again criticising the British - that is to say Mitchell-Henry's - sporting methods. This time M-H's exhaustive response was published in both the *Fishing Gazette* and his own book. Mitchell-Henry lambasted Grey for repeatedly failing to fish unaided, resigning his membership of the Tuna Club, his apparently contradictory views on light tackle fishing and much else besides, before ending on a familiar note: 'I cannot do better than to quote from his own account of his latest so-called record 1,040lb swordfish . . . a record no club worthy of the name would admit.'

Once again, and not for the last time, Mitchell-Henry was denouncing somebody else's record fish.

The dispute, it would seem, stemmed not so much from their differences, which were many and varied, but from their similarity. Both Mitchell-Henry and Grey had set themselves up as arbiters of international big game fishing rules. Unfortunately their views were diametrically opposed and neither of them were the sort of men to defer to another. Had they sat down in Pall Mall to discuss their differences, things may have been more civilised, but in the pages of the world's fishing press their respective reputations were at stake, and bitterly fought for.

Mitchell-Henry, of course, had many friends, some of whom were happy to fight his corner with him. Perhaps the most vociferous of these was Eric Horsfall Turner, whose critique of Grey was breathtaking: 'As Sherlock Holmes commented, it is of no consequence what you have done in the world. It only matters what you can make people believe you have done. If ever an angler filled this latter qualification of Holmes' comment, it was an American named Zane Grey. Mitchell-Henry shared my dislike of the angling charlatan.'

Mitchell-Henry's ire was not, however, reserved purely for his American rival. He was just as happy to make enemies closer to home, none more so than the organisation at the heart of the sport in Scarborough, the British Tunny Club.

Before the Tunny Club, the embryonic sport had been regulated by the British Sea Anglers' Society, who until the end of 1932 had issued certificates for tunny caught. For 1933, however, a turning point in the history of the sport, the new organisation assumed responsibility for ruling and regulating tunny fishing in British waters - and Mitchell-Henry was quick to denounce them.

The priority, as he saw it, was one of keeping tunny fishing on the highest ethical footing. 'I maintain that we must keep our sport on as high a level as any recognised rules that exist,' he wrote after the 1933 season. 'I consider that the standing of British sport is in question.'

Clearly, Mitchell-Henry had no confidence in the British Tunny Club's ability to keep the sport above board, with a large part of the problem being the number of fish caught outside the new club's rules. Referring to the Club's list of certified fish for 1933, he commented, 'It is frankly admitted that 79 tunny were caught by members of the club, yet only 19 of these can claim to have been caught under the club's rules . . . 60 fish (were) destroyed by methods outlawed by the club. Only one member of the committee which framed the rules appears in the list, therefore the numerous fish destroyed by other members of the committee are, on their own admission, murdered. There are several possible explanations for this act of unblushing hypocrisy.'

Mitchell-Henry was, in his typically forthright style, 'almost in entire disagreement' with the rules of the British Tunny Club. Rods, for example, could weigh 44oz but be only 4 foot 6 inches in length, a specification he felt was less than sporting.

Similarly, the rule allowing members to use a 72-thread line for
a year, as opposed to the standard 54-thread (a rule introduced
to mitigate the expense of those who had already invested in
the heavier line), was in his view far too lenient to be considered proper angling.

Other rules, such as rule six - stipulating that fish may not be
gaffed from a boat other than the one in which the angler is
situated at the time - did not go far enough. In Mitchell-
Henry's view it should have stated that a fish must be gaffed
from the boat in which it had been *hooked*, as any change of
boat should automatically disqualify a fish. The lack of a rule
limiting the permissible length of a gaff was, he felt, another
serious omission.

The British Tunny Club's rules, argued Mitchell-Henry at
length, did not seem especially interested in how a fish was
caught, and made the conditions under which they could be
caught far too easy. Quite how this equates with his complaint
that far too many fish were being caught outside the rules of the
club is not obvious, but on one point Mitchell-Henry is clear.
'The season of 1933 has proved in many ways a disgrace to
British sportsmanship,' he said. 'It (is) imperative that the self-
appointed British Tunny Club be dissolved, and that some
stronger body take over the control of the sport.'

For once, Mitchell-Henry did not get his wish. The British
Tunny Club continued to prosper without him, despite his
occasional broadsides in the angling press. He eventually grew
disillusioned with his tirades against the club, but resurrected
them with a vengeance in 1950, for yet another campaign - this
time a successful one - to have a record fish annulled.

By this time Mitchell-Henry had long since abandoned tunny
fishing in Scarborough - he had, after all, already enjoyed a big
game fishing career spanning four decades, and tunny fishing
had long since stopped being *new* - but he had changed British
angling forever. His influence on the sport cannot be under-
estimated, nor should it be diminished by some of the disputes

Mitchell-Henry with his 851lb world record.

in which he found himself embroiled. Yes, Lorenzo Mitchell-Henry may have been a dogmatic figure, overbearing and pedantic about the rules of the sport, but it was a sport which he almost single-handedly created. It should be remembered that before he turned up in Nova Scotia, with the tackle he had created himself, seventy-nine tunny had been hooked and not one had been landed. Mitchell-Henry, after a four hour tussle, landed the first one that he hooked.

Lorenzo Cecil Vaughan Mitchell-Henry died in 1965, just short of his ninety-ninth birthday. He was a remarkable man and had more than earned his footnote in angling history. Indeed, the time may come when he is given a more permanent memorial. A Scarborough pier came within a whisker of being named after him, but alas, a less esoteric choice prevailed. Had he still been around to fight his cause, the decision would probably have been a different one.

Ultimately, however, he got the only memorial he would really have wanted. Seventy-five years after he caught it, the official record for the biggest fish ever caught in British waters is still held by a Mr L. Mitchell-Henry, for a tunny of 851lb . . .

3

The Golden Years
1933 - 1939

Imagine the consequences of having luck on one's side!

The tunny phenomenon was no longer the preserve of a few friendly rivals. With the formation of the British Tunny Club, which by the start of the 1933 season boasted over sixty members, British big game fishing was now firmly on the map. It even had its own flag, as a brief article in the *Fishing Gazette* on 5th August, 1933 announced. The fledgling club had designed its own burgee, it said, a triangular flag featuring a tunny and the letters BTC. Members were told it should be 'flown at sea only when fishing, and not to be hoisted when entering port unless a fish is aboard'. Various sizes were available, from 2 foot for vessels of 5 tons up to 12 foot for those between 1,000 and 1,500 tons. It was impressive sounding stuff, although the *Gazette* felt obliged to point out that the new design was not actually a burgee, which is a swallow tailed flag, but a pennant. Whatever the nomenclature, it would become a regular sight returning to Scarborough and Whitby over the next few years.

Fittingly, given the mood of optimism that prevailed, the tunny arrived early that year. A wireless message from Lord Moyne to the Club's headquarters on 3rd August said that tunny were already plentiful on the northern edge of the

Colonel Peel off Scarborough in 1936.

Dogger Bank, some sixty miles away, and the following day Colonel Peel got the season underway with fish of 542lb and 459lb. His companion, Colonel Stapleton-Cotton, also managed a fish of 524lb, although his rod broke during the battle and he had to resort to hand lining, while both men lost several fish - which escaped with hooks marked by three file marks on the shank as part of the Club's ultimately fruitless attempt at tagging and tracking lost tunny.

Elsewhere in the North Sea, Lady Broughton landed a specimen of 564lb, although she had to hand the rod to her companion Lord Moyne after playing it from 11.25am until midnight, while Major Dugdale finally boated a fish of 467lb after a run of four porbeagle sharks. His son Eric also landed a slightly larger fish, bringing to an end a promising first week. With the seas calm and winds minimal, the British Tunny Club had enjoyed an auspicious start.

Mitchell-Henry, for his part, was determined to throw a small spanner in the works, and in the 12th August edition of the *Fishing Gazette* he was at pains to point out that, as yet, no tunny had actually been caught in 'British waters', namely within three miles of the low water mark. This was certainly true, but British or not, tunny continued to be landed at an impressive rate. By the beginning of September the *Gazette* reported that over twenty fish had been caught, with several notable captures among them. One of these was by Lord Egerton, who finally broke his duck with not one fish but two on the same line, while thirteen-year-old David Leigh came within 35lb of the then World Record - which was to fall a few days later to a 1,050lb fish off Nova Scotia - with a tunny of 763lb. His mother, Lady Leigh, hooked three fish, all of which broke away, while T.O.M. Sopwith and Mrs Sopwith also both caught. Meanwhile as the novices were catching their first tunny, old hands Mitchell-Henry and F. B. Hannam continued to do well, landing fish up to 728lb at Whitby. For them, though, the best was yet to come.

More and more new faces were turning up in search of a tunny, although the cost remained prohibitive. Ernest Schofield, an entrepreneur behind the Schoolboys' Own Exhibition at White City, thought he had the answer, offering tunny fishing from his converted Brixham mule, the *Leonora Minnie*, for two guineas a day. Tackle was not included but was available for hire from Harold J. Hardy at a reduced rate, minus lines and traces.

The North Sea had never seen anything like it and must have been peppered with tunny anglers. It was hardly surprising, then, that by 16th September the *Fishing Gazette* was reporting a 'record week for tunny'. 'Old Fuzzy' Clarke wrote to report over sixty fish landed between 19th August and 8th September, from a comparative lightweight of 325lb for Colonel Ashton up to fish in excess of 700lb for Colonels Stapleton-Cotton and Peel, T.O.M. Sopwith, A. R. Stobart, Mr Baker, F. B. Hannam and, after years of ill luck, Sir Digby Warren. It was a remarkable month, but the highlight came on 11th September when Lorenzo Mitchell-Henry landed a North Sea record of 851lb. It had fought hard for an hour and a half, and was an appropriate reward for the man who had virtually created sport fishing for tunny.

Mitchell-Henry was justifiably proud of his record, but far less pleased with what 'his' sport had become. Three years earlier, he had been a kindly father figure, generous with his help and anxious to assist newcomers to tunny fishing, but it had grown beyond his control. Clearly more fish had been caught than ever before, but it was the manner of their capture that concerned Mitchell-Henry. He suggested, in the *Fishing Gazette*, that the forthcoming list of fish caught in 'British waters' be divided into five categories: fish taken from row-boats; fish taken from yachts' motor-boats; fish taken on floats or pellets and lines; fish taken far out by yachts, trawlers and drifters; fish taken by local boats fishing from the shore. How else, he argued, could the 1933 season really be compared to previous years?

Mitchell-Henry was also concerned about overcrowding, and the declining standards of etiquette this brought with it. An angler who has located and baited up tunny, he argued, should be left alone until they have had a chance to hook a fish. He and F. B. Hannam, for example, had held back when they saw Major Rowley and Mrs Sparrow near a trawler, and were delighted to see both of them hook and land their fish. Conversely, when he and Hannam found their own trawler and started throwing herring overboard, six other anglers descended

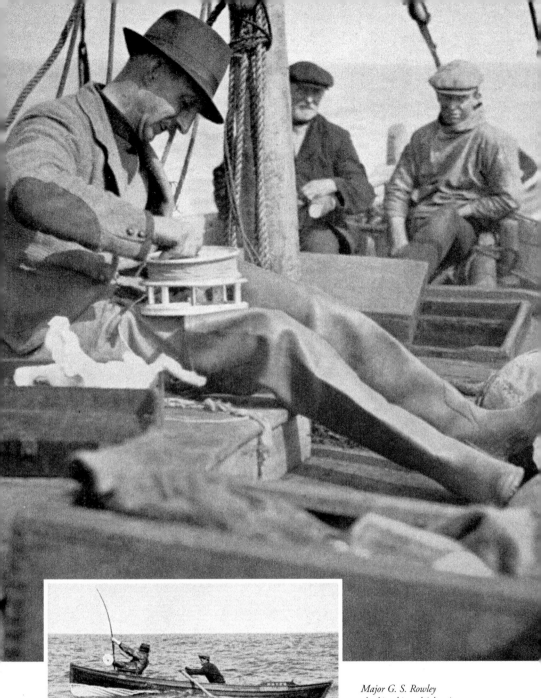

*Major G. S. Rowley
checking his reel (above)
and bending into a good
fish (left).*

on them with indecent haste. Their small area was now full of cobles and row-boats and 'there would not have been a 100-1 chance of getting clear' had a tunny been hooked.

Ultimately, many of the sport's new developments disappointed Mitchell-Henry. The strict rules of the game seemed to have been sacrificed so that anybody could turn up, catch a fish and call themselves a tunny angler. As proof, Mitchell-Henry cited the fact that of over sixty fish caught by members of the British Tunny Club, an organisation supposedly established to regulate the sport, only nineteen were granted a certificate. Far too many others had been shared fish, hand lined or otherwise captured outside the new rules. Mitchell-Henry branded these shenanigans a 'disgrace' and called for a much stronger organisation, possibly the BSAS, to take over for 1934.

He did not get his wish. The 1934 season dawned with the British Tunny Club stronger than ever and yet more would-be anglers arriving in Scarborough, keen to make their first ever fish a tunny. The title of Fred Taylor's new book, *Tunny Fishing for Beginners*, which was reviewed in the *Fishing Gazette* on 11th August, was surely a sign of the times.

The same issue reported the first tunny of the season, a specimen of 630lb captured from the *Silver Line* by Sir Joseph Hewitt on 5th August. Within two weeks the fish were present in abundance, with a 765lb tunny landed by Lieutenant A. H. Terry the largest of several caught. Colonel Peel reported that the fish were spread over a much wider area than in previous years, from twenty to sixty miles offshore, although they were 'in ones and twos only and no shoals, and are exceedingly shy of the bait - at least that is my experience'. It was an interesting observation, no doubt helped by the presence of F. S. Russell, of the Plymouth Laboratory, who was using Peel's yacht *St George* as a base for his tunny research.

Regardless of the small shoals, tunny continued to succumb to the growing flotilla of anglers. On 12th September Colonel Peel took a leviathan of 812lb, a fish that was initially attributed

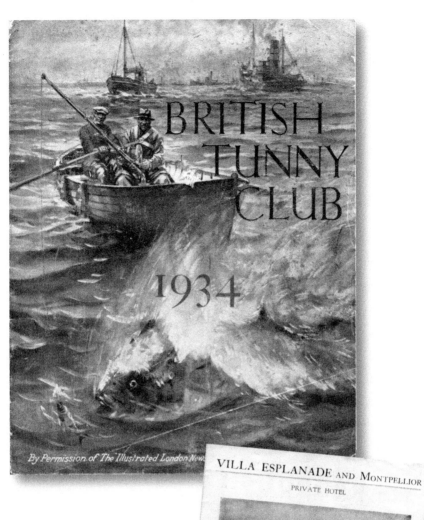

The British Tunny Club
Yearbook, 1934

[47]

Fishy Cartoons

SCARBRO' TUNNY
FRESH TO DAY. —

SWANK!

to Major Rowley in the press, while H. Giffard Smith, R. Hattersley-Smith, R. M. Ferguson, Fred Taylor and Tom Laughton were among several anglers successful later that week. Once again, tunny seemed to be caught with remarkable ease, leading to a cartoon in the *Fishing Gazette* showing a small schoolboy, complete with stick, string and proverbial bent pin, standing next to a large tunny. The caption said simply 'Swank!'

In Cornwall tunny were also being seen in large numbers, although these fish were generally estimated at less than 200lb in weight, leading some to speculate that they were a different species. Cyril Keen was the only angler to hook one, fishing a pilchard suspended beneath a pike float, but it broke his short conger trace and the mystery of Cornish tunny remained exactly that.

The 1934 season ended with twenty-nine certified fish, at an average weight of 616lb. No doubt to Mitchell-Henry's chagrin, a further twenty-five tunny were landed outside the accepted rules. It was an improvement on the previous season, but tunny fishing was still not the strictly-regulated game he hoped it would be.

The 1935 season arrived in spectacular style, with G. Heneage losing a huge fish. 'The season,' said Harold J. Hardy, who saw the beast, 'has definitely started.' Two days later Colonel Peel and N. D. Campbell both landed tunny, the latter's fish weighing 718lb, with R. C. Galloway getting another the following day. 'The sea is literally packed with them,' reported the *Fishing Gazette*. Peel went on to land six that week, up to 630lb, Campbell bagged a second, M. Wilcock Holgate and J. Wilcock Holgate Jnr got one apiece, while N. O'Halloran landed a brace.

Despite this success in the North Sea, talk of Cornish tunny still surfaced. Colonel Peel had spent a week that summer looking for them with F. S. Russell, and was nonplussed with what he found. 'We did not get a single report from any fisherman working these localities,' he wrote. 'I fancy the ordinary deep

Fred Taylor and his 707lb, 8' 3" long fish, which his boatman Bill thought was 'only a little 'un'!

sea fisherman is not a very reliable observer, and it is always possible Mr Le Gall or we have been misinformed. Anyway I am quite convinced, and so is Russell, that there are no tunny about within a reasonable distance of the coast here, and it would be useless for anyone to go to Cornwall in the hopes of sport yet awhile.' Shortly after his letter, however, a report from the BSAS said a shoal of reasonably large tunny had been spotted just 100 yards offshore at Logan Rock, Lamorna. Once again, though, nobody had actually landed one.

Later that month Fred Taylor telegraphed the *Fishing Gazette* to report that Mr Shepherd had boated a fish, although its weight was still to be determined, adding that the sea was 'alive with tunny'. Just days before he had sent a different message, stating that there was not a single tunny within 100 miles of Scarborough! Taylor had also been given a three and half minute slot on the BBC's 'Empire' programme, a time deemed 'painfully inadequate' to describe the thrills of tunny fishing.

The year ended with forty certified tunny, at an average weight of 563lb. A further thirteen tunny were landed but did not qualify for certificates, although D. Wilcock Holgate was awarded a Grey Seal for landing a 136lb porbeagle on 20th August. Sharks had long plagued anglers in search of tunny, and the British Tunny Club had obviously decided to recognise them as a sporting fish after all.

1936 opened with more talk of other species. The *Fishing Gazette* reported that Colonel Peel had started the season with a fish of 457lb on 6th August, with Lieutenant-Colonel J. R. Marryat adding a second the same day, but seemed more interested in rumours of swordfish in the North Sea. A Dutch drifter had had its nets damaged by large fish, with the skipper telling Harold J. Hardy he was convinced the culprits were swordfish. A further six tunny were landed from Peel's yacht that week, but nothing more was heard of the swordfish.

By 13th August, fifteen tunny had been landed, the biggest a

H. J. Hardy tunny fishing off Cornwall in 1934.

"Any tunny?" Jack Tansey approaches the trawler Kingsway.

Fish caught by H. E. Weatherley (2nd left) and Eric Horsfall Turner (4th from left) on 27th August, 1949. Fred Taylor is 6th from left.

638lb fish for Major Prior-Palmer, although weather conditions were ideal and the majority of fish were said to be within thirty miles of land. There were always exceptions, however, and Major Colin Cooper, of the Royal Thames Yacht Club, landed a 649lb fish eighty-five miles east of Flamborough Head. It was the first tunny to be landed at Bridlington, although it could hardly be said to have been caught there, and earned its captor a Gold Medal from the town's Mayor - who was no doubt keen to emulate some of the success Scarborough and Whitby had enjoyed.

Elsewhere rumours surfaced of a small tunny caught off Weymouth, with the *Evening Standard* claiming it to be 12 foot long and weighing 1¹/₂ cwt. Details were scarce, although the *Fishing Gazette* stated with some confidence that it was actually a 130lb fish, beaten into submission with oars by some passing conger fishermen, and was certainly shorter than the 12 foot claimed!

Back in Scarborough, Fred Taylor was cursing his luck. On 29th August he hooked a good fish but the hook pulled after thirty-five minutes, only to hook a second tunny soon after. This time the fish was fairly beaten after a tough three-quarters of an hour, only for the hook to break as the expired fish was being pumped towards the surface. Taylor said he felt there were plenty of tunny about, some twenty miles from shore, but the lack of commercial boats meant locating them was hard going. The *Fishing Gazette* bemoaned his luck on 12th August and wished him a change of fortune for the rest of his stay.

It obviously worked. Two weeks later, they reported just one tunny caught, a fish of 606lb for the very same Fred Taylor. The captor felt lucky to have had his fish, given that it was a lone specimen following a Dutch drifter. The helpful Dutch skipper had stopped and thrown free herrings to the tunny, which eventually made three passes at Taylor's bait before taking it. *The Hinckley Times and Guardian* shared this story with its readers, next to a report of a tunny exhibited in Burbage which was 'ten feet in length and weighed the better part of a ton'.

If the reported weight of the Burbage fish raised a few eyebrows, one can only guess at what the experts thought of comments apparently made by the Reverend R. D. H. Pughe, Rector of Burbage, on the tunny's habits. 'Two other fishes hate him - the whale and the shark,' he explained. 'Now you would think that he had no chance against these creatures, but like everything else it is given means to defend itself. When attacked by a whale or a shark it speeds away through the water at a great pace by means of those great fins. Then it stops suddenly and goes backwards towards its pursuer and tears its underside with this other fin.' Harold J. Hardy was so amused he sent the cutting to the *Fishing Gazette*, which dryly advised tunny anglers to beware 'reverse attacks of this description', and speculated, tongue firmly in cheek, that protracted fights with tunny may well have been fish travelling backwards, chasing sharks or whales.

Despite high hopes 1936 was a slightly disappointing year, with twenty-nine certificates awarded by the British Tunny Club. The most prolific members were Captain Frisby and Colonel Peel with a leash apiece and Lieutenant-Colonel J. R. Marryat with four, but the two biggest club fish, tunny of 765 and 753lb, were both taken off Nova Scotia by S. Kip Farrington. In home waters, nobody broke the 700lb mark.

One of the problems was the high number of tunny being lost, a trend highlighted in the new *Handbook of the British Tunny Club*. It was published at the start of the 1937 season, which began with several more tunny being hooked but not landed. 'It is to be hoped,' commented the *Fishing Gazette* on 14th August, 'that the inauspicious start of the 1937 season does not foreshadow a repetition of last year's losses.' In the same issue, Colonel Peel was said to have lost two tunny, one breaking his line under a trawler and the other doing the same under the keel of his yacht, the *St George*. Tunny were reported just fifteen miles off Scarborough, together with numerous sharks, but thus far nobody had landed one. With Fred Taylor vainly chasing tunny in Cornwall, 1937 was not looking promising.

It was not until 12th August that the duck was broken, when Major W. F. Henn landed a tunny of 707lb. Initial reports suggested that the rod had broken during the fight, meaning the fish would not earn a certificate, but it later emerged that Henn's rod had broken on a second tunny of 591lb. The season had started at last, and for several weeks tunny followed in reasonable numbers. W. W. Dowding took four fish up to 648lb and Captain Frisby boated five, although Henn's fish remained the biggest tunny of the year.

If 1937 had been a difficult year, 1938 was another season where everything fell into place. By 9th August, Harold J. Hardy had written to the *Fishing Gazette* with a brief report on the first five fish of the season, all of which had fallen to the indefatigable Colonel Peel's party. The Colonel himself had managed a brace of middleweights, while J. M. Peel, R. M. Peel and J. Barclay had each managed one apiece. The North Sea was cloaked in fog, said Hardy, but the waters were calm and he signed off 'in haste' to take advantage of the improving conditions.

Hardy was soon sending in more catch reports. The tunny were close to shore, some within three miles of Scarborough, and feeding hard. On 21st August five fish were shared between four anglers, with Colonel J. A. C. Whitaker enjoying a brace of 562 and 553lb. On the following day Whitaker got three more, with Captain Frisby landing a fourth, while on the 23rd eight tunny were boated, including leashes for Colonel Peel and Captain Mathews. No tunny were landed on the 24th, but the 25th and 26th saw a further thirteen tunny, including a quartet for Captain Frisby. Clearly, the tunny were present in huge numbers, and H. R. Jukes regaled listeners of the 'Northern Programme' with his experience of being surrounded by

H. J. Hardy with a fish on.

Mr Hardy with a 684lb tunny.

200 feeding tunny while aboard a trawler near the Dogger Bank.

1938 was already a bumper year, but the highlight came on 1st September. Captain Frisby, who had already landed seven tunny during August, boated five fish for a total weight of 2,812lb - the biggest haul of North Sea tunny ever taken in a single day. It was the most remarkable performance in a record-breaking year, and by the time Colonel Sparrow landed a 587lb fish on 11th September, the British Tunny Club had handed out no less than forty-one certificates. With good weather and no interruptions, 1939 could well have been the greatest tunny season ever . . .

Scarborough holiday snap from the 1930s.

Obviously it was not to be. By September 1939, tunny fishing was no longer a priority for a group of anglers whose collective identity was so rooted in the armed services. In all, ten fish were landed that year, but only Harold J. Hardy qualified for, or took the trouble to apply for, a British Tunny Club certificate. It was to be the last legitimate fish of the sport's golden years. The tunny were still out there and the anglers would eventually return, but for now tunny fishing was effectively on hold. Soon, boats would be scarce and the North Sea would become a far more dangerous place . . .

4

Tackling a Tunny

*There came a rushing swirl of water, a splash and a
glimpse of triangular fin. A huge, glittering blue and
silver shape shot past under the surface with
incredible speed, and the herring was gone.*

With the discovery of tunny in the North Sea, a whole new
branch of angling was born. Tunny were not just larger and
more exotic than British anglers were used to, but demanded
different methods to land them. It was not, as Eric Horsfall
Turner explained, 'a matter of taking a small boat to sea, with
suitable tackle and hope'. It was a much bigger undertaking,
not dissimilar to the siege tactics being developed in moun-
taineering at that time, employing many men to put just one or
two on the summit. Tunny fishing was an expensive business
that promised what Horsfall termed 'considerable difficulty and
discomfort.'

The fish itself, however, had a weakness that the early pioneers managed to exploit when developing their methods.
Tunny, above all, were hungry creatures, opportunists that had
to scavenge in order to achieve their enormous proportions. No
predator could ever have grown as large as a tunny without a
ferocious appetite, in this case for small and agile fish such as
herring and mackerel. Even a middleweight tunny would need

huge numbers of herring to sustain it, and the North Sea had not only herring in abundance, but a fishing fleet that dished them up in a remarkably convenient way. In effect, the North Sea's drifters and trawlers were ground-baiting for tunny on a colossal scale. 'One can imagine that the netted herrings,' wrote David Carl Forbes some years later, 'a veritable mass of dislodged scales and phosphorescence, provided a mammoth "rubby dubby" as the nets were hauled.'

It was no wonder, then, that the herring fleet were the first to spot the North Sea's tunny population, or that they were to play a central part in the tactics employed by anglers to catch them.

The first objective for any tunny angler was to find the fleet. Casual readers of the angling press may have thought the North Sea was alive with tunny every August and September, but the North Sea, as Fred Taylor once remarked, is a big place. It was not just a case of finding a tranquil spot of water and pitching a herring overboard. The tunny would be miles away, hounding the trawlers and waiting for the nets to be hauled. W. Stanley Sykes, in *Harness of Death*, described the process in typically florid tones: 'The crew of the trawler spat on their hands and began to haul in the weed-encrusted net. Narrower and narrower grew the triangular bag of it as it was hauled in. Shining, silvery forms came into view above the water and slipped back into the cod end or extremity of the net at the next pull from above.'

It was as the nets reached the surface, with thousands of herring thrashing in an ever decreasing circle, that the tunny's feeding frenzy reached its height. If an angler could find the fleet at the right time, get close to one of the marauding tunny and drop a baited hook in its path, then a hooked fish was suddenly a real possibility.

Getting to the fleet in the first place, however, was the first challenge. A boat was required, and a small industry thrived on the east coast as a result. 'There are at present two kinds of motor boats for hire at Scarborough,' wrote Fred Taylor in 1934, 'one which is called a coble, which is an open boat about thirty-five feet long, and the other kind, called a keel boat, which is a much larger boat, decked over. A keel boat has one great advantage over the smaller boat, in that you can cover more ground, and go much further out. As things are at present, an open coble, which is what I use, and which is the cheapest form of tunny fishing you can get, costs £21 a week - this includes the services of two men.'

This was in the early days, however, and by 1950, prices had risen. An open coble of between thirty and forty feet, capable of fishing up to twenty miles from port, could now be had for £42 a week, while a forty to sixty foot keel boat would set the angler back £70, plus expenses. A third option was also offered, a larger steam drifter, and while this cost considerably more it was able to carry several anglers and stay out to sea for extended periods.

In the first few seasons, the majority of fishing was done using cobles, within what Taylor termed a 'reasonable distance' of land. 'What I mean by reasonable,' he explained, 'is within, say, fifteen miles of land; forty miles out or so can by no stretch of imagination be called reasonable. Of course tunny sometimes come in much nearer than fifteen miles. I hooked one last year within four miles of the shore, and there were several other fish round our boat at the same time.'

As time passed, and ever larger vessels were employed, other anglers' definitions of reasonable went far further than Taylor's. By the mid-Thirties, many thought nothing of chasing tunny some 100 miles from land, despite the extra costs this incurred.

The actual fishing itself, however, was not done from cobles, keels or steamers. They were too unwieldy to intercept fast moving tunny, and ill-equipped to chase a running fish. Instead, for an extra £5 a week, or £12 by 1950, the angler could also hire a small rowing boat which would be towed out to the fishing grounds. This was adopted as standard practice,

A Dutch herring boat.

A Yorkshire coble. This is the Geoffrey, often used by Fred Taylor.

A trawler hauling its nets.

with the angler and a boatman quickly switching to the smaller boat when feeding tunny were found. The rowing boat also had the added advantage of acting as a weight for the hooked tunny to pull against, and while the rod could not be attached to the boat itself, according to British Tunny Club rules, if the angler was determined enough and could hang on grimly, the effect was much the same.

The tackle, of course, was unlike anything British anglers had used before. It had to be. Nobody really knew how large a tunny could grow - as late as the 1950s, Tunny Club literature was speculating *when*, not *if*, the first 1,000lb fish would be caught. Clearly, conventional sea fishing tackle would be woefully inadequate.

A rare consensus agreed that the reel was the single most important item of tackle. It was the reel, as Taylor noted, that was placed under the most stress in the initial stages of a fight: 'It is hopeless to try and stop the fish on his first rush (which is the longest). Pretty well all you can do is stop your reel overrunning. This must be done at all costs.' To survive this early onslaught, the reel had to offer sufficient breaking power. Traditional capstan or star-drag reels were used by some, but they had no quick release mechanism and many anglers preferred an auxiliary drum brake, easily adjusted by means of a long lever. Colonel E. T. Peel, for example, had one added to his reel for the 1934 season, with remarkable success.

Peel, like many others, used a Hardy Bros. reel. Hardy had a long association with Scarborough's tunny anglers, not least because Harold J. Hardy was the company's representative in the town, and developed many items that were to become standard Scarborough kit. The 9-inch version of Hardy's Fortuna, for example, introduced in 1923 as a development of their Tuna Big Game Reel, was perhaps the most popular winch in the North Sea. Most were built using Duralumin by Arthur Humphrey Wall, and reels bearing the AHW stamp were as sought-after in the Thirties as they are collectable today.

The Fortuna, though, was not without its critics. 'It is undoubtedly a very high class reel,' commented F. B. Hannam, 'but, being friction-driven, it will slip if any really great strain is put on it . . . although I have known of very large fish caught by Mr Ramsay at Odden with this reel, I do not know exactly how these fish are held by the reel unless the brake is jammed, which is not a safe thing to do.'

The Fortuna remained popular, however, although Hardy's American-market Zane Grey model also had its devotees. Like the Fortuna it was a highly-engineered device, and novelist Sykes was so impressed when he saw one that he included a description in *Harness of Death*: 'The whole thing was reminiscent of a motor car in its sturdy complexity, and, like a car, had to be lubricated with a special grease gun.'

Lorenzo Mitchell-Henry, not unusually, did things his own way, building an eponymously-named reel that offered perhaps the best alternative to the Alnwick company's range. It was certainly a fearsome weapon. 'I expect many of our members smiled up their sleeves,' wrote F. B. Hannam in the *BSAS Quarterly*, 'when they first saw Mr Mitchell-Henry's huge reel. In our room at Headquarters, it did indeed seem monstrous. Far out at sea it was quite the reverse. It then seemed to me that the entire outfit . . . should be at least twice the size.' Typically, however, Mitchell-Henry had tested it with his usual thoroughness, lifting a 250lb dead weight in order to gauge its braking power. On occasions, it seemed as if he were more interested in the reel than the fish it was meant to capture. Hannam once watched him play a 413lb tunny to the gaff in three-quarters of an hour, only to ignore it when it was finally hauled aboard: 'He was taking no interest in his prize. He was down in the fo'c'sle with his precious reel. He had taken it apart and was looking quite carefully at the interior. "Come up and look at your fish," I said. "Come down and look at my reel," was the reply.'

Mitchell-Henry eventually added a second handle on the

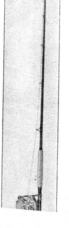

HARDY'S TACKLE
for TUNNY FISHING

has been used in the capture of most of the World's Record Big Game Fish. You cannot do better than follow the example of experienced and successful anglers by using tried and proven gear.

For Particulars, Prices and Hire Terms, apply

HARDY'S ALNWICK, LONDON, MANCHESTER, EDINBURGH, GLASGOW
Or to HARDY'S BRANCH, SANDSIDE, SCARBOROUGH

The 9 inch "FORTUNA" Big Game Reel, with Auxiliary Hand Brake; for holding and pumping heavy fish

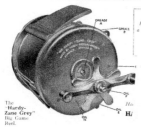

The "Hardy-Zane Grey" Big Game Reel.

By Appointment to The Late King George V

By Appointment to The Prince of Wales 1931-36

USE

HARDY'S
TUNNY
TACKLE

Hardy's are the pioneers in the production of
TUNNY GEAR

Practically all the tunny caught since the commencement of the sport in the North Sea have been taken
on
HARDY TACKLE

HARDY'S . ALNWICK . ENGLAND

LONDON	EDINBURGH	MANCHESTER	GLASGOW
61 Pall Mall	69 George Street	12 Moult Street	117 West George Street
12 Royal Exchange			

13

THE ALLCOCK TUNNY ROD

No. 8745

No.
8745. Suitable for all Big Game Fish this rod is made from a special alloy steel, hardened and tempered, giving a tensile strength of 95 tons per square inch. After rustproofing the weldless steel is finished off with clear cellulose. Line guides are hand-made from highest quality stainless steel and are sweated directly on to the rod. The combined line and harness ring is of brass : it is detachable, and its position may be adjusted to suit the user. Although far stronger than anything made in built cane, hickory or greenheart, this rod (which consists of a top and a short butt) has sufficient resiliency to safeguard the tackle, giving just the correct amount of whip and perfect recovery which is essential. Prov·   ·he butt for the screw bolt of the Allcock reel to pass   ·rity. Although especially designed for ·   modate almost any Tunny reel.   tongue of the No. 8745RR Rod   rod. The measurements of the r   Tunny Club's regulations. Leng
£8 15s. 0d.

N.B.—This price includes one 87

No.
8745RR.

The record Tench (7

TUNNY TACKLE—contd.

TRACES

No.
8470. The '' Mitc ·
highest qu·
reinforced :
with specia
corrosive st
Suitable for

8411. The '' Allcoc·
lighter trace
have no hesi
used.'' **12 6**

8814/2x. The '' Mitcl·
steel wire wi
eye. This is
length 6 inch

8414. The '' Mitchell-H·
used by many w

5252MH. See page 110.

Never, neve·

TUNNY AND BIG GAME
FISH TACKLE

THE '' ALLCOCK-TUNNY '' REEL
(Patent No. 446598).

No.
8946. Made under licence from Mr. L. Mitchell-Henry, the tunny fishing pioneer and captor of the world's record tunny (851 lbs.). This new model has many great advantages over any other reel of this class, including a positive drive which cannot slip, combined with a handle which upon being released becomes instantly free so that it cannot spin and endanger the angler's hands. It possesses also a most effective '' Ferodo '' hand brake, sensitively controlled and of amazing strength. An adjustable drag is provided which permits the line being trolled behind the boat without revolving the reel, but which may be instantaneously freed if desired. This is of the utmost value when a shy fish is playing with the bait. The main portion of the reel is made of Duralumin, which has strong anti-corrosive properties. Diameter of drum, 7 inches. Line capacity, 36 thread 570 yards ; 54 thread 430 yards. Weight (approximate), 7 lbs. 14 ozs. **£18 18s. 0d.**

A detailed specification will be sent to any angler on request.

Allcocks have been making fishing tackle exclusively for 134 years

216

opposite side of the reel so that the angler could wind with both hands when pumping a tunny up from the depths. The British Tunny Club did not allow a second handle for its certified fish, but as Mitchell-Henry had nothing but contempt for their rules, it would have made no difference to his design.

Whichever reel was used, it would have been easily the most expensive item in the tunny angler's armoury. A tunny rod would have cost roughly half as much as the reel, but it was a rather more contentious topic. Mitchell-Henry summed up the choices objectively enough, but soon struck a more characteristically provocative note. 'The tip may be of split cane, greenheart, hickory, ash or other suitable wood,' he wrote, 'my personal preference being for lancewood, which I have found the most satisfactory.' At the time there was a general preference for split cane, not least because it was what most of Hardy's rods were built with, and Mitchell-Henry couldn't resist drawing attention to the number of split-cane rods that disintegrated *in extremis* during the 1933 season.

Mitchell-Henry declared himself 'by nature, reluctant to say I told you so', but went on to do exactly that. Had the unfortunate anglers only followed his example, as previously detailed in *The Field,* he gently chided, and used a lancewood or greenheart rod made by Mr Pritchard of Scarborough, they may have escaped with both rod and pride intact.

Hardy Bros, for their part, also knew a bit about fishing rods, and continued to build theirs from split cane or hickory. Perhaps the most suitable was the No. 6 Salt-Water Palakona, a 6-foot 10-inch weapon boasting a formidable 42lb test curve, Hardy's 'over and under' roller tip ring and a detachable hardwood handle. They also offered a more sporting No. 5 version with a mere 35lb test curve, for 'light tackle' tunny hunters. It is interesting to note that Col. E. T. Peel owned both and when his rods came up for auction recently, the lighter rod seemed to have enjoyed much the less use of the two.

Given the relatively small numbers of tunny anglers, Hardy

worked hard at cultivating their custom. As soon as tunny were caught off Scarborough adverts appeared in the angling press, telling readers the sort of tackle they could buy to catch them. The adverts tended to follow a similar theme throughout the tunny years, combining pictures of impossibly large fish suspended next to their stunned-looking captors, with photographs of Hardy's big game products spread liberally over the rest of the page. The September 1931 advert showed Fred Taylor with his 735lb British record, Harold J. Hardy with his marginally less impressive 392lb specimen, and the 6-inch Zane Grey reel and 9-inch Fortuna models they used. The image of the former helpfully showed the six points on the reel which required the regular application of either grease or oil.

The advert struck a suitably triumphant note, explaining that 'The wise angler who is determined to try for the giant tunny this season will, after listening to and reading all the arguments about tackle, buy the gear which has been successfully used by the most famous and expert Big-Game Fishermen in the world, ie. gear made by Hardy's.'

Subsequent adverts played on a similar theme, although some did at least tell aspiring tunny anglers how much the tackle would cost them. In August 1933 they were offering a steel-centred Palakona No. 6 at £12 one shilling and sixpence, or a hickory version at £5. A Zane Grey reel, capable of carrying 450 yards of 54-thread line, was priced at £30, while the slightly less capacious Fortuna was just under half the price.

Casual readers may have thought Hardy had a monopoly on tunny tackle, a perception the company was keen to encourage. In August 1937, they placed an advert in the *Fishing Gazette*, claiming the vast majority of tunny were taken on Hardy gear. Mitchell-Henry's Scarborough rod maker, Mr Pritchard, was as quick to put pen to paper as his client. 'In the current issue of your paper,' he wrote, 'appears an advertisement claiming that nearly 100 per cent of tunny caught in British waters have been taken on tackle supplied by this firm.

Hardy ads from 1931.

I consider this an unfair, incorrect and misleading statement. Many tunny have been caught on tackle other than that advertised, by the following anglers: Mr Mitchell-Henry, Lord Egerton, Sir Digby Warren, Sir Joseph Hewitt, Col. Sparrow, Mrs Sparrow, Mr Hannam and others. Col. Peel has caught twenty tunny on two rods made for him to replace those of other makes that failed. I have also replaced broken rods, not of my make, for the following gentlemen: Mr T. O. M. Sopwith, Mr Sigrist, Col. Stapleton-Cotton, Capt. Frisby, Col. Peel. In each case I have obliged the angler by using the fittings off their broken rods . . . are the fish caught by these anglers credited to the rods or the fittings?'

While the rod and reel were perhaps the most debated tackle choices, not just because of their origin but also their cost, they were of little use to an angler unless he or she were comfortable while afloat. 'Sound seating is a primary factor in enabling the angler to outfight the fish,' commented Mitchell-Henry. 'It is almost impossible to succeed, as at least one fisherman has experienced, if one is using recently developed blisters as hydraulic cushions between oneself and the boat.' Sadly, Mitchell-Henry chose not to reveal the identity of the angler for posterity, but anyone who has spent a few hours on the unforgiving thwart of a rowing boat can sympathise with the luckless posterior in question.

A harness was also essential. Fred Taylor felt that 'no living man could fight one of these fish without it', and wisely nobody seems to have tried. 'There is no stopping the first run of a tunny, it is far too large and powerful, and incredibly fast,' added Tom Laughton. 'The reel screams and the pressure on the point of the rod is so great that the angler can only keep it up by bringing the harness into play.'

Fighting a tunny, advised the normally understated Eric Horsfall Turner, 'entails from thirty minutes to two hours of the most gruelling, back-breaking strain to be met with in any sport, with the possible exception of the annual Boat Race between Oxford and Cambridge'. It was only by fighting a tunny with the whole upper body, and firmly braced legs, that the angler stood any chance. A well-designed harness allowed them to do just that. Hardy Bros. offered tunny anglers its 'Scarborough' harness, made of military-style webbing, with separate straps for fishing the reel under or over the rod (a choice that also seems to have divided anglers into very distinct camps). The harness featured a safety release mechanism on its straps, an essential device designed to prevent a hapless angler, tethered to his rod, from being dragged overboard if his reel seized.

Dragging a well-upholstered tunny angler overboard, it might be added, would require some fairly substantial line. Fortunately the tunny fraternity had several brands at their disposal, most of which looked, according to Horsfall Turner, 'like white parcel string, but immeasurably stronger'. Initially, lines were classified, following the American fashion, by the number of strands rather than their breaking strain. A dry breaking strain of 2lb was assumed for each thread, giving

*Left: A 1912
Big Game outfit.*

*Below: Mitchell-Henry's
1926 tunny outfit.*

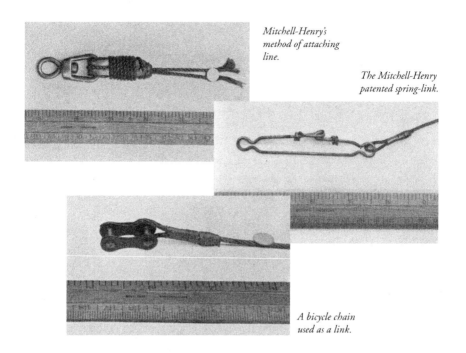

Mitchell-Henry's method of attaching line.

The Mitchell-Henry patented spring-link.

A bicycle chain used as a link.

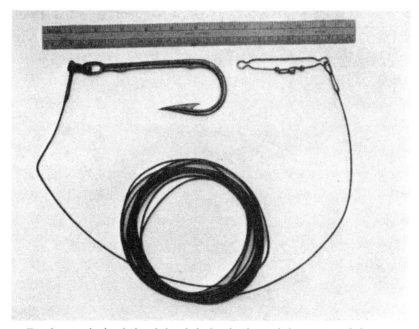

Typical trace with a bicycle chain link to the hook and and spring link to connect to the line.

nominal breaking strains of 144lb and 108lb for the most commonly used 72- and 54-strand American lines. Mitchell-Henry, however, whose 851lb record was caught on the latter, was quick to point out the futility of rating lines this way, citing a British-made 63-strand line which had a measured test of over 250lb. To his mind, the strength of the line was less important anyway, in sporting terms, given the inability of any angler to place a direct pull of 108lb on a fish, than the total length of line used. If line length were unlimited, he felt, anglers might let a fast-moving fish run to the extent that it was tired out not so much by the pull of the rod, but the weight of the bow in the line. The angler would then have nothing to do but take up the slack in a leisurely fashion, by which time the fish would be exhausted without battle ever truly being joined. For a sportsman as combative as Mitchell-Henry, this was anathema.

The choice of terminal tackle was mercifully free of controversy, by tunny fishing standards. A trace was invariably used, with Hardy's Scarborough Trace - 25 feet of 500lb b.s. twisted steel cable - being fairly typical. Hooks of various patterns were legion, mostly between four and six inches in length, although some lures, including Hardy's Silver Herring Tunny Bait, were offered for sale. Few if any tunny, however, are thought to have succumbed to artificial baits.

Little else was needed to catch a tunny, other than chartering a coble and rowing boat, but the prohibitive cost of tunny fishing tackle was hotly debated. Sykes, who researched *Harness of Death* in the company of Fred Taylor, was in no doubt that here was a rich man's sport. 'Hundreds of anglers would give ten years of their lives to do this,' remarked one of his characters, 'only they can't afford it. [There was] a display of tunny tackle which amazed Drury by its price. One outfit, stated to contain everything requisite, was priced at fifty-seven pounds.'

The British Tunny Club agreed, suggesting that tackle should cost an aspirant angler between £40 and £60, although it did point out that it could be hired instead. Indeed, by 1950, when according to George Baker it was 'almost impossible to buy new tackle as most of it is still going for export', the Club had acquired three sets of Hardy tackle, which it hired out for £4 per day or £12 for a full week.

Even so, a week's tunny fishing remained far beyond the reach of the ordinary working man. Some small economies were possible, and even the affluent, yacht-owning Peel saved a few pounds by catching many of his tunny on traces made of ordinary Bowden cable, bought for three pence per foot. This was a token saving, however, and of little consolation to anyone who found the cost of a rod, reel and boat prohibitive.

Eric Horsfall Turner, comparing tunny fishing to fine art, summed it up best. 'Like all the great pictures,' he said, 'its purchase has been expensive from the outset.'

Even for those able to afford the tackle, the real challenge of persuading a tunny to take the bait remained. While the drifters and trawlers acted as a focal point for the fish, the anglers then had to do their own localised ground-baiting in order to bring the quarry within reach of tackle that was incapable of casting a bait in the conventional way. The baited hook was free-lined within a few yards of the rowing boat, or suspended from a bamboo pole, and the oarsman would try to keep the small boat in the vicinity of the feeding tunny. Meanwhile, on the coble or keel boat, somebody would throw in free offerings to keep the quarry near the surface, often plugging herrings with corks to keep them from sinking.

If this complex sequence of events somehow came together, the tunny would boil, much the same as a trout in its final struggles, according to Horsfall Turner, and a take was often immediate. 'Now is the time to hold your breath,' advised Taylor, 'because anything may happen as soon as your bait hits the water. Suddenly the air becomes electric, as a great shout goes up - "There he is!"' But a take was never inevitable. 'They are knowing brutes,' he added, 'and it is indeed tantalising when

A tunny comes aboard for Major Rowley.

they seem to take every fish thrown to them, except the one that is on your hook.'

The whole enterprise was a remarkable one, and all the more so given that it often happened at night. The continental drifters were at work during the day, but the East Coast fleet more usually worked in darkness. If anglers were to catch tunny as the British fishermen hauled their nets, they would have to do so with only the commercial boats' deck lights to guide the way. It was a challenge many anglers were keen to take on. 'It is quite practicable to make a night search with a Yorkshire coble,' said Horsfall Turner, 'starting from Scarborough around 11pm and getting among the herring fleet about 1.30am. Skipper Tom Birch, though now retired, has put many an angler into a tunny by this method.'

For their part, the commercial fishermen were generally happy to help out where they could. A sense of co-operation prevailed, the anglers making their way from one set of lights to another with the standard call of 'Any tunny?' A case of beer often changed hands, in return for either information or a basket of herring to use as bait, particularly if the trawler or drifter announced it was about to haul. If it wasn't, or no tunny had been seen, the process would be repeated at other boats until both feeding tunny and an imminent haul were found. On at least one occasion, a trawler was happy to do an unscheduled haul to help out a no doubt generous tunny angler. 'The fishermen, on the whole, are a very decent lot,' said the angler in question, Fred Taylor, 'and if they see any tunny about, or are about to haul, they usually give blast on the siren.'

Tunny fishing was never an easy business, either physically or logistically, and the methods seem rather convoluted to today's convenience-minded anglers, but somehow it worked. Quite how the well-heeled anglers, the taciturn Yorkshire men and the foreign herring crews rubbed along so well together, however, remains one of the more charming mysteries of the tunny years.

5

Thunnus Thynnus

*I have watched them by day in a clear sea, moving
beneath our craft like dark green ghosts.*

The twenty-first century fish is a known commodity. Science
has blown its cover and unravelled its secrets. The ferox trout,
for example, remains an enigma, but echo sounders and
tagging have made it more tangible, less elusive. Carp -
considered uncatchable during the tunny years - are now old
friends, complete with nicknames. The tunny, however, is still
almost as mysterious as it was when it first appeared off the
Yorkshire coast.

Indeed, nobody really knows when the North Sea tunny first
showed up. Unlike many big game fish, they don't tend to
advertise their presence by leaping about. Their daily lives are
conducted well below the surface, but the herring industry
changed that, at least for a while. 'In an average year,' estimated
Hugh Stoker in 1956, 'no fewer than 1,680,000,000 of these
little fish are landed at the ports of England, Scotland and Wales
alone.' Small wonder, then, that the tunny were tempted to
poke their noses above the waterline when the commercial
boats hauled their nets.

Exactly how long the tunny had been lurking there, however,
is anybody's guess. Indeed, Eric Cooper (author of *Modern Sea*

Cutting up the tunny. From Gerhard, Aus.Vas., *plate 316, 2.*

Fishing: from Bass to Tunny, 1937) felt that anglers' ignorance of tunny in home waters was proof of how little they actually knew. 'We need only consider the case of the tunny to realize how much there still is to be learnt about the fishes of our seas,' he argued. 'Here is a fish that probably has always been a migrant to Irish, Scottish, North Sea and the waters off Cornwall, yet only during the last half dozen years have they been discovered by anglers.'

This was despite the fact that the first known report of a tunny from the British Isles came as early as 1769, at Inveraray, where Pennant recorded a fish of 460lb.

'How is it that they have only been found so recently?' Cooper continued. 'The work of the eminent French biologist, Monsieur J. Le Gall, first focused attention on the real possibilities, when a map he prepared showing the distribution of the tunny round the British Isles was published. In this he marked areas off the Scilly Isles, around Scotland and in the North Sea.'

Once the tunny's presence was finally confirmed, British anglers were quick to see its sporting potential. Here was a fish quite unlike anything else in our waters. Fred Taylor, in 1934, neatly summarised its physical appeal. 'If you examine a tunny you will observe it is a wonderful lesson in streamlining,' he wrote. 'As an example, the dorsal fin fits down into a groove, about the thickness of your finger, so that it is perfectly flush with the body when folded down. The pectoral fins are recessed, and another curious feature is the two small finlets which stick out at right angles to the powerful tail. The shoulders are immensely powerful, and a good sized fish will measure well over six feet in girth at this point.'

But where had it come from? And where did it go for the ten months or so that it wasn't within reach of Scarborough's cobles? Before long, tunny 'experts' were making educated guesses, among them the inevitable Mitchell-Henry. 'It would appear that the tunny come in the spring from the Atlantic,' he stated with typical authority, 'and first show themselves off the Scilly Isles . . . on reaching south of Whitby and Scarborough, they appear to turn eastwards out to sea, and knowledge of their movements ceases at this point.'

Fred Taylor, author of the only other major book on tunny during the Thirties, could add nothing more. 'It is a curious fact that the tunny seem to stop at Scarborough,' he mused, 'and, as far as I am aware, hardly any tunny have been seen south of a point due east of Flamborough Head.' He, like Mitchell-Henry, had no idea where tunny disappeared to each September.

Mitchell-Henry, however, was frustrated at this lack of knowledge and trawled European records to fill in the gaps. He found that tunny were seen off France, Spain, Portugal, Norway and Denmark at various times, usually materialising in European waters in May, only to disappear again in June before making a final appearance in August. He also speculated that water temperature and salinity were behind their seasonal excursions,

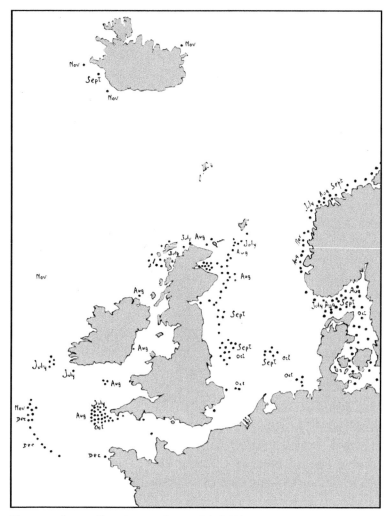

Tunny were often seen if not always caught around the British coast.

particularly as spawning approached, and dismissed the idea, suggested by some scientists, that tunny were actually warm blooded creatures.

Much conjecture focused on the tunny's migration routes. The prevailing view was that tunny headed north from the Mediterranean and North African coasts as temperatures in

Northern European waters rose. Certainly, they were only found in water above 10-12 degrees Centigrade, and a cold summer in the North Sea would mean a late start to the tunny season.

Tunny were also found off Cornwall, although these fish were generally smaller and were never captured using Scarborough methods. Fred Taylor, for example, tried several times without success, and was one of several to suggest that Cornish tunny were actually a slightly different species. In *Big Game in British Waters*, Captain W. S. Kneeshaw summed up what was known, or thought to be known, about them: 'These fish make their appearance off Cornwall in July and remain until the temperature of the water falls, often as late as November. During this period it is believed they chiefly frequent the area off Land's End.'

Kneeshaw dubbed the Cornish tunny 'elusive' and repeated the oft-heard regret that they had never been taken on rod and line, but did recall one small fish, of 56lb, taken on a hand line while making its way up the river Fal. He didn't try to explain this strange behaviour, but suggested that most Cornish tunny would eventually make their way around Ireland and over the Orkneys, before reaching the North Sea. Sadly, he offered no evidence for this idea.

Professor Massimo Sella, *Directeur de l'Institut de Rovigno d'Istria*, made the first scientific attempt at charting the tunny's movements, by tagging twenty small specimens caught off Gallipoli. Not one of these fish was recaptured. Undaunted, Sella started dissecting tunny caught in Sardinian stake nets, retrieving ingested hooks and trying to locate their source. He enjoyed some small success, identifying hooks used by long-line fisherman in Tarifa, off the Spanish coast. Thus encouraged he continued to make sporadic progress, although his various conclusions never amounted to a coherent thesis, and he strongly urged fisherman to adopt national markings on their hooks in order to further his studies.

Sella's suggestions found support from some in the North Sea tunny fraternity, with the fledgling British Tunny Club keen to investigate the idea. In 1933, F. S. Russell, Naturalist at the Plymouth Laboratory, spent two months aboard Col. E.T. Peel's yacht the *St George*, where he hoped to further the work of Le Gall, Sella and 'Old Fuzzy' Clarke. Plenty of fish were caught by Peel and his friends, and Russell was able to make painstaking measurements of thirty-two tunny in all. He noted some slight differences between the fin placements of his North Sea fish and tunny measured in Tunis by Heldt and off the Algarve by Frade, but his main thesis focused on Sella's idea of tracking migration through lost hooks. With support from the Tunny Club he was able to identify five types of hooks left in lost fish - two from Hardy, two from Mustad and a Pritchard model - and devised a scheme of marking hooks through three saw cuts or punch marks on the shank. Quite how the anglers felt about potentially weakening hooks meant to hold tunny in excess of six hundred pounds is not recorded, but the Tunny Club were apparently very co-operative, and Russell recorded that 'a more detailed system of marking . . . might be used in future years should the method prove successful.'

Others were more sceptical, particularly the Tunny Club's main detractor, Mitchell-Henry, who pointed out that lost tunny with 6- or 7-inch hooks and steel traces attached to them were unlikely to survive long enough to be recaptured, or in sufficient numbers to make any scientific conclusions worthwhile.

Mitchell-Henry was right. By the end of the North Sea's tunny era, anglers were really no further forward in understanding the fish's movements. As late as 1972, eighteen years after Scarborough's last tunny, David Carl Forbes commented: 'Tunny are enigmatic fish: huge, truly oceanic creatures . . . constantly confusing those scientists who would trace their migratory jaunts throughout the seas.'

Whatever their origin, the tunny were just as enigmatic for Scarborough's residents, who flocked to see the leviathans when

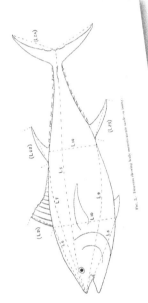

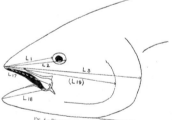

*Pages from Russell's
report in 1933.*

Three tunny caught in the North Sea, 4th August, 1933, hanging from the side of the
M.Y. St George. *From Russell's report, photograph taken by Victor Hey.*

they were brought to the scales. 'The Major', a fisherman and stalwart of 'The Newcastle Packet', opposite the Tunny Club's old headquarters, recalls paying a penny as a young boy to see tunny displayed in a green hut by the harbour - although many somehow evaded the admission fee, or sold herrings dropped at the quayside to pay for it. The profits were given to the crew or went to a local charity, initially John Bamford's East Coast Cot Fund or latterly the Scarborough Tunny Charity Fund, but this too was far from ideal. Fred Taylor's 735lb tunny was displayed in a marquee on the understanding that half the proceeds would go to his boatman, but £30 of the £35 were taken with expenses, leaving £2 10s to be shared between the hapless recipient and his crew. In all, they each received just twelve shillings and sixpence.

Nevertheless the practice of displaying a decaying tunny for a paying public continued, much to the annoyance of F. B. Hannam: 'A more wasteful method of dealing with such magnificent and valuable fish food is difficult to imagine, while the action of the local authorities, for the gain of a few pounds . . . is to be deplored.'

Once again, Lorenzo Mitchell-Henry thought he had the answer. 'The question of the use of tunny for food I consider of very great public importance,' he explained. 'I have already roused some public interest . . . the budding canning industry will, I hope, find increased turnover by dealing with this fish.' He was not alone. Col. E. T. Peel also advocated the commercialization of tunny fishing and in 1938, with war already looking inevitable, he wrote a long letter to *The Times* outlining his thoughts:

The article in your issue of September 9 under the heading 'Herring in Wartime' calls attention to the importance of North Sea herring as a regular, and more particularly as an emergency, food supply. With the same object, attention might also be directed to tunny, which nature in recent years has brought to our shores in such abundance. Tunny fishing is carried on in the Mediterranean and other parts of the world as a national industry of considerable importance. I am convinced that this class of fishing could be profitably exploited in the North Sea if a home market were to be created. From July to October tunny appear in immense quantities near our shores, and can easily be taken by simple methods on quite inexpensive tackle calling for no outlay of capital. Moreover, trawlers and drifters working the grounds could make good catches with little or no interruption of their normal work. The fact that a party with me fishing for sport were able to take 20 fish in three days, aggregating about 5 tons, furnishes striking indication of commercial possibilities. This is a heavier weight of fish than would normally be landed by a Breton tunny boat after an eight to 10 days' trip working some 200 to 300 miles off shore. A North Sea trawler or drifter properly equipped with hand tackle and using proved methods might reasonably be expected to take on each trip 40 to 50 fish averaging 550lb., while a smaller craft working exclusively for tunny should make much larger catches. Thus a large and regular supply of fish could be assured for the market during the season. Tunny as a delicacy and form of staple diet has been used for centuries. The canning process is cheap and simple. The product in oil keeps for years. Surely so rich a harvest, offering employment to our North Sea fishermen and valuable food supplies, should not be neglected.

Of course, Peel was unlikely to change the nation's dining habits from his armchair at the International Sportsmen's Club, on Upper Grosvenor Street. Nor was he the first to try, although Mitchell-Henry, the most vocal supporter of canning tunny, had taken a more practical approach. In 1932, he provided local fishermen with sturdy hand lines with which to capture any tunny that followed them. The hand lines worked well enough, but when Whitby-based trawler *Pilot Me* succeeded in catching two tunny for food, including one of 812lb, an anonymous poet, using the *nom de plume* Lucio, was moved to write a poem to the *Manchester Guardian*:

Oh, shame on Whitby's ancient port, and shame upon the skipper
Who treats a tunny pretty much as though it were a kipper!
He puts a common hand-line out, the undistinguished bounder -
The sort of tool one uses for a codling, plaice or flounder!

Stands Whitby where it did, gadzooks? Are tunnies what we fancied?
Ah, no - when caught like this I fear their fame is rather rancid.
But what about the sporting code? Aye, there the worst of shocks is -
A tunny on a hand-line, sir, is worse than shootin' foxes!

Mitchell-Henry, to his credit, printed this riposte in his book. And besides, just occasionally, somebody would take his advice and try to cook a tunny. Perhaps the most memorable such occasion was in 1938, at the Trocadero Hotel, although in retrospect, cooking the tunny whole may have been a mistake. The fish in question, a 731lb specimen taken off Tommy Sopwith's *Vita*, was added to 200 gallons of water, 30lb of salt and a healthy dash of carrots, onions and bay leaves. According to *The Times*, it took three hours for the concoction to reach boiling point, after which it was left to simmer for ten hours. The plan had originally been to cook the fish on the roof of the hotel but, as the chef apparently remarked, 'You can't carry it about like a whitebait.' Instead, it was prepared in the kitchen.

When the tunny was eventually squeezed through a serving hatch, the hotel presented it whole, with hot tunny at the head end and cold, iced tunny towards the tail. As *The Times* wryly noted, this could never have been done with a herring.

Despite such culinary excesses, the North Sea's tunny never really found a domestic market. Fred Taylor, for example, felt it had little culinary merit, remarking: 'I had some sent to my club - I understand some of my friends did not exactly rave about it,' while novelist W. Stanley Sykes, in *Harness of Death*, took a swipe at a supposedly fictional character who was determined to turn the tunny into an industry: 'There is one gentleman who wants to commercialize it - the last fish he

Tunny steaks selling in Scarborough for 3d each.

caught weighed five hundred and sixty pounds, and it sold in the market for eight pence a pound. But most of them don't like it. They say it'll spoil the sport and start the big boats harpooning them.'

Mitchell-Henry was not named in the novel, but given that he sold at least one 560lb tunny in Harrogate, and was the loudest voice in the case for the tunny as a food fish, we can safely assume the identity of the gentleman Sykes was alluding to.

Even the atavistic Captain Kneeshaw, who recommended hunting seal, grampus, pilot whales, dolphin, porpoise and just about any living creature without a decent public school education, conceded that commercialising tunny fishing would not be easy: '[It] is so well established a sport as to be an industry in itself. I think that the fishermen would rather resent any attempt to commercialize it. This, I know, was the case when shortly before 1939 an attempt was made to supply East Coast fishing vessels with a light harpoon gun, similar to that used by

Norwegian fishermen, on very generous terms. The fishermen, however, were too satisfied by the fees earned taking out tunny fishers to take any interest in the offer and the vested interest won, but circumstances alter cases and it is possible that the future will bring changes in their outlook.'

Kneeshaw would certainly have welcomed such a change: 'I have no doubt that a light harpoon gun . . . would meet a long filled want and be a valuable piece of equipment for anyone who is frequently single and wants some weapon not too cumbersome and expensive when out fishing. I should have been glad of one more than once myself.'

In 1957, three years after the last tunny was caught on rod and line, the likes of Mitchell-Henry, Hannam and Peel finally got some culinary backing. Food writer Ambrose Heath called the tunny 'more of a curiosity than a dish in this country,' but published recipes for grilled tunny, braised tunny and stewed tunny fish *bonne femme*. Then again, Heath also suggested baked weevers as a credible dining experience, so maybe we should add a large pinch of salt to his recipes after all.

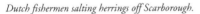

Dutch fishermen salting herrings off Scarborough.

6

Tunny Tales

*Harrison had a wild desire to fish. Never before had he felt
the least inclination . . . but this was a man's job, and
the full blooded vigour of it appealed to him.*

Tunny fishing seemed to have galvanised society like no angling trend had before. 'Why, then, the tremendous fuss over North Sea tunny?' asked Eric Horsfall Turner in *Angler's Cavalcade*, 'Was it vanity, or was it the equivalent of Everest, or the North Face of the Eiger?' Whatever the reason, each year, increasing crowds of newcomers invested a great deal of time and money in getting themselves a tunny. Many were anglers who simply fancied a chance of something larger than the brown trout they had caught from the Test, but others had never held a fishing rod before in their life.

Some debutants, such as amateur steeplechase jockey Laurie Kirkby, of Barton-upon-Humber, did rather better than the more seasoned campaigners. A friend of J. A. Tansey, stalwart of the British Tunny Club and captor of many a good fish, Kirkby was invited aboard the keel boat *Shirley Williamson* to see what tunny fishing was all about. Tansey himself had recently enjoyed a run of five and six hundred pounders, but his friend was about to eclipse him.

Their first night was a blank. Ports had been closed after a glut of herring, so no nets were being hauled. Without trawler activity to attract the tunny, there was no hope of finding fish, even such large fish, in the featureless expanse of the North Sea. But luck was on their side. Tansey and Kirkby travelled to Whitby the following morning, only to hear that ports were being reopened for a 10 cran quota. Boats would be out, albeit not for long, so that night they followed the herring fleet to sea. Tansey lost three fish in the dark, fishing off a Fraserburgh drifter, while Kirkby entertained himself watching phosphorescent tunny gliding beneath their boat.

At first light, after a forty minute battle, Tansey got his first tunny to the gaff. With such small herring quotas, however, most of the fleet were already heading homewards. Just two remained, a drifter and a Dutch 'honky tonk' vessel, so the two friends chased after the drifter for a final throw of the dice. It was Kirkby's turn to strap on the harness, if they could only find a tunny for him to try for . . .

As Kirkby savoured a much-needed cup of tea in the wheelhouse, crewman Charlie suddenly screamed 'tunny boil astern'. Kirkby and Laurie Williamson leapt into the rowing boat and a baited herring was soon in the water. For an hour and fifty minutes, the tunny would only take free offerings, fastidiously avoiding the one with a hook and trace attached. They tried suspending the bait on the surface using bamboo rods, then fishing it deep, but neither worked. The fish was still there, however, so they held back on the loose herrings and within ten minutes, the tunny's greed got the better of it.

'That poor fish was under the whip,' wrote Tansey in his log, 'and kept under until the battle ceased 25 minutes later. This tunny weighed 703lb and is the heaviest fish landed here this season.'

Kirkby rode Limber to win two point-to-point races later that day, leaving his host to reflect on the fact that in fourteen years of chasing tunny, he had never caught what Kirkby managed to hook within two hours of first holding a rod: a fish over the 700lb mark.

Jack Tansey hauls one aboard and (below) his 526lb tunny of 1947.

Tansey lands another and (below) his huge catch of 31st August, 1949.

* * *

Tom Laughton, owner of Scarborough's Pavilion and later Royal hotels, was made to wait rather longer for his first fish. Harold J. Hardy was a frequent guest at the Pavilion, and suggested that Laughton give tunny fishing a try. A gastronome, hotelier, self-confessed womaniser and brother of actor Charles, Tom Laughton was not a man who had spent his life saying no. He chartered a decked coble, Tom Pashby's *Our Maggie*, and set off in search of his first tunny.

Laughton chartered the *Our Maggie* for a full four weeks, but for the first three, they chased the herring fleet around the North Sea without seeing a sign of a tunny. Their lack of fish was disappointing but, as Laughton noted in his biography, tunny fishing - even unsuccessful tunny fishing - was a compelling diversion from his other life: 'It was an interesting new experience, leaving the harbour, setting a northerly course past the Scarborough Castle Hill, with the lights of the town receding in the distance. Then, as it grew colder, going into the smelly cabin with its small, glowing stove, having a cup of 'char' made with condensed milk, and gradually getting to know the crew who were a sturdy lot, full of fun, and just as keen as I was to get a tunny.'

Unsurprisingly, the gregarious Laughton became friends with some of the drifter skippers, particularly on the Dutch and Scottish boats. One of them was Billie Normandale, whom Laughton memorably described as 'a plump little man, who wore a bowler hat green with age, and whose hail came over the water in the form of a magnified "ginny" whisper.' It was Normandale who they came alongside one evening, asking the by now perfunctory question, 'any tunny?' The skipper stuck his bowler-hatted head out of the wheelhouse and smiled. Not only had they seen fish, but the tunny were actually following them.

At that moment, Tom Pashby spotted a black dorsal cut the surface between *Our Maggie* and the drifter. Laughton and his oarsman, Charlie, got into the small rowing boat and, as the last light faded, the tunny took Laughton's proffered herring. Its first run towed them well away from the *Our Maggie* and before they knew it they were fighting a big fish, at night, with no sign of their parent vessel. 'We were on our own,' wrote Laughton, 'in the mist and without a lantern in our boat. It took me four hours to bring that fish to the gaff and most of the time we were lost to the *Our Maggie*. By the time Tom found us I was completely exhausted. I wanted Charlie to give me a knife to cut the line, but he wouldn't. All he would say was "Hang on, hang on."

Laughton suddenly remembered that he had a flask of brandy aboard the *Our Maggie*. Tom passed it across and thus fortified, Laughton was able to bring the 600lb fish to Charlie's gaff. They returned to Scarborough just after first light. It had been a close run thing, for Laughton had only two days of his four week charter left.

* * *

Tom Laughton aboard the Our Maggie.

Laughton's 1947 leash of tunny.

Tom Laughton knew full well, however, from some of the tunny anglers who stayed at his hotel, that he had been lucky to succeed so soon. One such guest was Lord Egerton, who stayed at the Pavilion in the early Thirties. For two full seasons, he stayed in Scarborough, fished hard and failed to land a tunny. The third year looked like being a similar failure, until right at the end of his stay he landed not one tunny, but two simultaneously - one of which got its tail caught in his line as he played the other.

That evening, he was dining alone in the hotel and called Laughton over. "Do you know," he told him, "this is a wonderful moment for me. I have had a dreadful time, I hate the sea, I am a shockingly bad sailor, but I had to have a tunny for my big game museum. Thank God I have got one at last - you will never see me again."

Lord Egerton, as a gentleman, was as good as his word. He took his brace back to Tatton Park, the Cheshire family seat, and was not seen in Scarborough again.

* * *

Tunny anglers, it seemed, were a tough breed, despite their often pampered upbringings. On one occasion, Kaj Moeller, then holder of the Danish tunny record, finished a dinner party at midnight, changed and drove the seventy-five miles to Odden, set sail before 3am and returned at first light with a fish of 400lb. He then drove home that morning, keen to make a luncheon party at midday. Such tiresome obligations as sleep, it would seem, would not get in the way of a tunny, food or a social engagement, something Mitchell-Henry would have heartily agreed with. As Hannam once said of him, 'the man who can face eggs that should have been hard boiled but were not quite hard, at 3.15am, and follow them up with bread and jam, is made of the right kind of stuff'.

Some other would-be tunny anglers, however, were rather less stoical. In 2002, a collection of tunny tackle appeared at auction in London, in remarkably fine condition. The lot included a No. 6 Hardy Palakona big game rod, a Fortuna reel filled with Olympian 54-strand line, a Zane Grey gaff, a bamboo and brass outrigger pole, a Scarborough big game harness, various hooks, traces and a macramé twine finger stall, all in two purpose-built zinc-lined pine boxes. The unnamed original owner had apparently invested in this state of the art outfit and travelled to Scarborough in 1934, only to suffer a debilitating attack of *mal de mer*. After a few hours this gentleman angler asked his skipper to return to dry land, where he put the new tackle in storage, never to be fished again.

* * *

Even for more enthusiastic sailors, tunny fishing was never an easy business. For every heroic tale of big fish landed, there are several more of huge fish lost to anglers left bruised by the encounter. There are also just as many stories of futile hours on a hostile North Sea, vainly searching for drifters or trawlers, struggling to find the unique combination of circumstances under which a tunny might be hooked.

'One bitter memory I have,' recalled Fred Taylor, 'was when I left shore around 2am, and we got to the drifters around 4.30am and found everyone had hauled up their nets and were full steam ahead back to Scarborough. I hope none of them overheard any of our remarks . . . the language was somewhat lurid.'

Even when he did find tunny, and Taylor hooked plenty over the years, there was no guarantee that they would make it to the boat. On one memorable occasion, after several barren days, his line went slack while playing a good fish, and the result was one of the more florid laments to a lost fish: 'Oh ruddier than the cherry, I quoted in disgust, as I consigned the entire family of tunny, both great and small, their fathers and mothers, sisters and brothers, wives, sweethearts and concubines (or whatever it is they keep), to the utmost depths of the nether-world. Slowly I wound in my slack line.'

Fred Taylor waiting aboard the Agnes.

Fred Taylor, his skipper, Tom and Brian (Taylor's son).

Fred Taylor bends into the 707lb tunny before his seat broke.

After the accident, boatman Bill hangs on to Taylor's seat as the fish is landed.

To Taylor's surprise, however, after reeling in some 200 yards of line, the fish was still on, and a fight ensued in which the strain of the battle actually broke his boat's seat in half - leaving him in the unenviable position of being tied to a rod which, in turn, was attached to a fish more than capable of dragging him overboard in a flash. The boatman Bill's reassurance that this fish was 'only a little 'un' seemed strange some hours later, when the tunny weighed in at 707lb.

It had been a close call. Tunny fishing was potentially a dangerous activity, as F. B. Hannam was keen to point out. 'The knowledge of the fact that one is engaged in a sport involving a very great amount of danger is, I hope, a sign of intelligence and not cowardice . . . The man who will not take every precaution while endeavouring to take the life of an opponent of twice, or it may be, four times his weight, had better insure that life heavily so that someone may benefit by his stupidity.' To make his point, he related the tale of an early tunny angler who had fixed a rope around his waist but omitted to tie the other end to the boat. His reel overran and he was being dragged overboard to an inevitable watery death when, with the intervention of providence that protects 'fools, drunken men and anglers', the tunny ran under the nearby launch, cut the trace on its propeller and saved not just its own life but that of its would-be captor.

Of course, the North Sea was quite dangerous enough, without any help from the tunny. Anglers frequently raced for port as weather worsened, but the desire for a fish would sometimes overcome good sense. In 1932, Major Rowley spotted a tunny during a heavy swell and took to the rowing boat, ready to do battle, only for his skipper to refuse point blank to allow one of his crew to join him.

Fortunately it was only in a work of fiction, W. Stanley Sykes' wonderfully silly detective novel *Harness of Death*, in which the dangers of this new sport were fully realised. Sykes wove an improbable but entertaining tale of a power struggle between two ruthless gangsters, one of whom spent much of his ill-gotten gains chasing tunny: 'Marston was a man of expensive tastes...and had spent considerable amounts on his new hobby. The thrills and excitements of this wonderful big game sport threw into the shade all lesser fish. Once Marston had tasted the mad rush of a six hundred pounder, his one object in life was to repeat the experience as often as possible.'

Marston eventually attempted to murder his business rival by taking him tunny fishing with a doctored harness, which would send him to a watery grave should he hook a fish. Ridiculous hokum, perhaps, but it allowed Sykes, who joined Fred Taylor on one of his tunny jaunts by way of research, to indulge in the sort of adjectival purple prose that more restrained angling writers rarely used: 'His mouth was dry, his hands blistered. Every muscle in his body was racked with an intolerable ache; he was gasping for breath and his arms were trembling and his legs shaking from the long-drawn strain of the battle . . . In the last split second as the boat turned round Harrison saw a cold, implacable eye glaring up at him out of the water; saw also a huge scar on the back of the fish, a relic of some long past, grim battle for food or a mate in the soft green darkness of the sea.'

One can hardly imagine Lorenzo Mitchell-Henry, or the colonels and captains of the British Tunny Club, waxing quite so lyrical.

* * *

One might equally wonder what some of them made of the many female anglers who tried, often with great success, to catch a tunny. Surely such a tough, sometimes dangerous occupation as tunny fishing would be some sort of floating gentleman's club?

Fred Taylor thought so, at least at first. 'Thank goodness,' he reflected in 1934, 'we have at last found something at which women can't compete with us men . . . was said in all good faith to a friend of mine, soon after we had commenced tunny fishing. [But] once again, man's supposed stronghold has fallen. There are now ladies - Mrs Sparrow, who was the first lady to catch a tunny here, and that well-known sportswoman, Lady Broughton - who have entered the sacred precincts, the holy of holies, the *sanctum sanctorum* of the committee of the British Tunny Club.'

As well they might. Female anglers may have been a minority among the tunny fraternity, but they caught more than their share of fish. The first success was Mrs Sparrow, with a fish of 469lb in 1932, but this was only the beginning. The following season, noted big game hunter Lady Broughton managed a brace of certified fish, weighing 553 and 523lb, while Mrs Sopwith, Mrs Stancliffe and Miss Yule all gained red seals - which were awarded in 1933 only, for fish between 500 and 800lb. Of nineteen fish awarded certificates in the British Tunny Club's debut season, no less than five fell to female anglers - an impressive feat for such a small minority.

1934 saw Lady Broughton back in action with another brace of fish, the biggest of which was a true giant of 738lb. September also saw a fish landed by Miss Dora Walker off Whitby, but its capture was hardly within Tunny Club rules. Miss Walker had set out in Skipper J. R. Storr's *Pilot Me* on the Friday night, accompanied by her brother, Colonel James Walker, and early the next morning they found a shoal of feeding tunny. Rough seas meant the small rowing boat could not be launched, so they fished with hand lines from the tender. Colonel Walker lost two fish before boating the third, then his sister hooked a tunny which almost found sanctuary in the nets of a nearby trawler. She prevailed, however, and they headed back to Whitby. Curiously they were followed back to port by several tunny, some of whom ate melon rinds thrown to them from the *Pilot Me*.

When the seas settled down the Walkers tried again, this time fishing with rod and reel from the small boat. Colonel Walker hooked and lost a good fish, but Dora didn't get her chance at a legitimately-caught tunny.

The following two seasons saw few North Sea fish fall to female anglers, but elsewhere in the world, women were doing well. The world record for a tunny caught by a woman was beaten twice in 1937, both times off Nova Scotia. On the first occasion, Mrs Earl Potter boated a 757lb specimen using equipment borrowed from well-known American big game fisherman - and British Tunny Club member - S. Kip Farrington Jnr. She subdued her fish in just over two hours, before continuing her holiday cruising Canadian waters. Her record lasted only a day, however, until Mrs William Chisholm, of Ohio, took a tunny three and a half pounds heavier. The new record fish, which was 9 foot 8 inches long with a girth of 6 feet 4 inches, took just fifty minutes to beat - a time that would have been impressive for the most robust of male anglers.

Back in England, Mrs Joan Baker and Mrs Kathleen Sutcliffe boated fish of 383 and 644lb respectively, the latter winning a bottle of Williams & Humbert's Dry Sack Sherry for her trouble.

With the resumption of post-war tunny fishing in 1946, Miss Maureen Lees tried for a tunny from Michael Wild's steam yacht, *Georgiana*. Her first tunny made good its escape beneath the keel of a Dutch drifter, but she soon hooked a second. 'Miss Lees, an attractive brunette,' gushed the *Fishing Gazette*, 'had had no previous tunny experience. "It went away in a great flurry," said Miss Lees, "and the small boat from which I was fishing went swirling through the water with it. There was a tremendous strain on my rod, but the line held securely, and it was a wonderful moment when I realised on my first trip I was to be successful." '

The fish weighed 507lb, earning its captor a Grey Seal Certificate and the Ward and Terry Trophies from the British Tunny Club, but in 1947 an even younger angler, eighteen-year-old schoolgirl Miss Bidi Mary Wild, did even better.

Fishing with her brother, Michael, from the same yacht used by Miss Lees the year before, Miss Wild hooked her tunny within quarter of an hour of getting into the dinghy and landed it just half an hour later. It weighed an impressive 714lb.

One or two anglers, led by Mitchell-Henry, felt that tunny fishing was not quite the physical contest it was said to be, and schoolgirls landing seven hundred pound fish in short order can hardly have convinced them otherwise. But some observers were still amazed that women could go toe to toe with a tunny, not least novelist W. Stanley Sykes. A character trying tunny fishing for the first time in his *Harness of Death* remarked that 'Rugby football's a parlour game compared to this. One or two women have done it. Must be regular Amazons - all wire and whipcord.' Sadly, even the *Fishing Gazette* doesn't record quite how Amazonian Miss Lees and Miss Wild were, but Sykes was obviously impressed.

While Sykes may have created a romanticised, fictional view of tunny fishing, the reality was every bit as colourful. One anonymous correspondent chose to share his experiences, if not his name, with readers of *The Times*:

At this time of year that romantic enigma, the Atlantic tunny, pays a visit to our East Coast in pursuit of the herring shoals. Imagine an opalescent dawn in the North Sea out of sight of land. A few drifters whose lights we have been following begin to loom up, reminding some of us of the bad old days of mine-sweeping. The sea is grey and oily and there is a slight swell. Nets are being hauled, but there are few herrings and no tunny. But suddenly from a mile away one of the fishing-boats looses a succession of agitated blasts of his siren. We hurry to the spot. He is hauling up long lines well garnished with cod. Yes! he shouts in broad Yorkshire, 'a coople o' tooney' are playing around. You seize the rod and with your harness on your back, like brave Horatius, leap into the rowboat we have been towing, followed by the boatmen with a box of herrings. In the meantime the owner lowers his dinghy and sends a hand across to the Girl Annie with his thanks for hooting and Will the

Master accepts a handful of Dutch cigars and returns the compliment with a live cod.

While these high-sea courtesies are in progress and you are adrift and forlorn in a small boat rowing for Girl Annie, all at once the sea divides and a great grey back with scimitar fin emerges. No! not the tunny, but a herring whale some 60ft. long. He lounges gracefully across your bows with a knowing leer and emitting a gargantuan sigh, disappears. His companion surges up to investigate the yacht and so they continue playing, feeding, and sighing within a biscuit's throw. You must keep your hook out of their mouths, only praying that they do not elect to rise beneath your inadequate craft. 'There he goes!' yells Girl Annie and as you come alongside you discern a dark porpoise-like shape that rises to take the herrings flung by willing hands. You bait him freely from your box, trailing the treacherous hook before his very nose. At last he is tempted and takes the bait quickly down with a sudden impressive swirl, the slight check on the reel being sufficient to drive the hook in. The line screams out and now is the anxious moment. Will he dive under the Girl Annie and foul her lines or propeller? But no! Your luck is in, he is off for the open sea! Cheers from Girl Annie and cheers from the yacht, for you are well hooked into the fish of a lifetime, and if your gear holds and your luck - not to mention your stamina - you may bring him to the gaff. His first run is a moderate one and it is only when you tighten up that he shows his strength in a wild 150-yard dash. Your boatman follows, and presently, checking him as much as you dare, you have the pleasing sensation of being towed over to Holland by a big fish! And so it goes on, pull devil, pull baker, hour after hour, until the great fish weakens and is brought near the boat. Still some dangerous bids for freedom to be countered, and then suddenly he comes alongside - dead. He is hoisted on to the parent ship which has been anxiously following you and you climb on board, a physical wreck maybe, but treading on air, for you have got your fish. There he is, a good 500lb. weight of green and silver suspended by his tail from the masthead shining in the morning sun. "Not bad for a hors d'oeuvre," says the owner.

F. B. Hannam was another angler driven to flights of fancy by tunny fishing. In his BSAS article 'Tussles with Tunnies', he admitted how he had once, during a long fight with a good fish, imagined a conversation between the tunny and himself: '"I have just come up to have a look at you, and I don't think much of your judgement to come out here at your age with such a thin little line and funny-looking blunt piece of wood to try conclusions with me." My reply was: "I am afraid you are right, old chap, but, as man to fish, I don't mind telling you that if you would only tear out the hook or swim back faster than I can reel in and cut the line with your tail, I shall consider you are doing me a good turn. You see it is this way; the orders of the BSAS are that I must fight on until you beat me, so the sooner you do it the better I shall be pleased." "Right, off I go; thanks for the tip."'

With such drama on offer, it was hardly surprising that when Tom Laughton returned to Scarborough after the war, it wasn't long before he was lured away from his hotel and back to chasing drifters. Tom Pashby, still the skipper of *Our Maggie*, called to ask whether he still had his tunny fishing tackle. Once again, Laughton found it impossible to say no, and they were heading out into the North Sea.

'Tom was steering - as pleased as I was to be on the tunny hunt again,' recalled Laughton . . . '"It won't be as long this time," he said, "they were telling me on Saturday that there are hundreds of tunny about, go below and have a kip - we shall be fishing as soon as dawn breaks."'

Quite whether Laughton was able to sleep in his excitement is not known, but just before dawn, he was indeed donning his harness under the deck lights of the herring drifters that surrounded their small boat. Soon the trawlers began to haul and they made their way from boat to boat, surrounded by blowing whales, searching for tunny. Within minutes, a distinctive fin cut the surface. Tom Pashby handed Laughton the rod, a herring was swung out and the take was immediate.

Within an hour, his first tunny was alongside, in Laughton's words 'nearly as long as the boat'. As the crew hauled it into the *Our Maggie*, Laughton cast again and within half an hour, hooked his second fish. The sun was still low when he hooked his third fish of the morning. 'We were back in the harbour by mid-day with three fish aboard,' wrote Laughton. 'I was completely done, my back was aching, my arm muscles throbbing, all I wanted to do was get into a hot bath. So I made tracks for home, leaving the three huge fish almost covering the deck of the *Our Maggie*.'

'Later that afternoon,' he added, 'the telephone rang; it was Frank Watkinson, the secretary of the Tunny Club. "You are wanted down at the harbour," he said. "The press want to take your photograph with the three fish." "What do they weigh?" I asked him. "Five hundred and thirty-six pounds, seven hundred and seven pounds and seven hundred and eighty-five pounds." "Good God," I said, "there won't be room for me in the picture."'

* * *

One of the most staggering tunny catches, however, was made by Captain C. H. Frisby, in 1938. For once, here was a total catch which could be weighed not just in pounds, but in tons - one and a quarter of them, to be precise. His tale is worth hearing in full, for all his habitual understatement:

I left Scarborough at 12.20am in the MV Albatross, *a keel boat, skipper Bill Pashby, on a north-east course. From 4am onwards we spoke to various Dutch herring drifters, but to our cry "Any tunny?" there always came the cry "No tunny," and they were proved correct as we could not bait any up, though we threw in herring while lying alongside each of them. At last, at about 7.15am, we found a drifter which had had tunny with them when the nets were hauled.*

I got overboard into the small boat and within ten minutes was into a fish which I killed in thirty-three minutes, hauling the tunny into the keel boat at 8am. He weighed 621lb. While killing this fish another Dutchman steamed up to talk to the first drifter and he brought tunny along with him.

I was quickly into the second fish, but he took me an hour and twenty-three minutes and weighed 527lb.

Having on August 26 killed four fish in one day, my skipper, Bill Pashby, was very keen for me to beat that number, and in addition we both felt that if we could kill five fish of the weight we were getting, the day would be a record hard to beat.

So, breakfastless and rather tired, I again went overboard in the small boat to the second drifter.

Captain C. H. Frisby

I was soon into a fish, the third, and this I killed in thirty-seven minutes - weight 461lb. A double whisky and off again. I was soon fast to another fish, but unfortunately, after five minutes, he doubled back and went under the drifter. I felt the line touch the keel, but got clear and the fish forged ahead and took out all but about fifty yards of my line. I tightened well into him, but snap! and the line broke close to the trace. This seemed the biggest fish so far, but he got away.

I put on a fresh trace and was into my fifth fish within fifteen minutes. This fish, after a 200-yards run, also escaped me, the line again breaking. It had obviously been damaged in more than one place against the drifter's keel. Meanwhile, both drifters steamed away, but two friends, Mr H. W. Kempston, a member of the British Tunny Club, and Mr H. Phillips, who had come with me as spectators, managed to take the tunny away with the Albatross when the drifters left, by feeding them

with herrings, of which I had over 1,000 on board. I changed my reel and line and put on a spare one with a new trace, and was quickly fishing again against my own keel boat.

Mr George Baker also came along from M Y Joanna, *and we were both soon fast into fish, my sixth. After about five minutes our lines crossed, but we managed to get clear and we both killed. This sixth fish, the fourth kill, took me thirty-two minutes and weighed 658lb.*

The time was now about two o'clock in the afternoon and there seemed to be no more tunny by the keel boat, so after a short and much needed rest, I went off to a drifter in the vicinity and after about twenty minutes was into my seventh fish, and after thirty-two minutes killed it, making a total bag of five. This fish weighed 545lb and was hauled aboard at 3pm.

These fish were all caught between thirty and thirty-five miles north-east from Scarborough. They were all brought aboard alive and kicking and there was a good deal of excitement each time one was hauled up and lowered on to the deck, as each fish, averaging quarter of a ton, crashed up and down on the deck and one nearly knocked out one of the crew who got a crack on the point of the chin from a tail.

However, they were all secured, the row-boat hauled on board, and then off for home, arriving at Scarborough at 8.45pm. I cannot speak too highly of my boatman, George Bayes, whose skill with the boat contributed a great deal to the success of the day.

My skipper, Bill Pashby, I consider second to none in his happy knack of finding tunny, and he is an expert in handling the trace and gaffing the fish. He and his crew work like Trojans all day, and their pleasure at the outcome of the eight hours' fishing made the effort all the more worth while. I can confidently recommend Bill and the Albatross to any angler who goes to Scarborough to try for tunny.

* * *

Of course, for every red letter day, there were those the tunny anglers would rather forget. Fred Taylor, whose tunny career lasted longer than most, knew this better than anyone. On one memorable occasion, with Tom Pashby in attendance, he had a day just as remarkable as Frisby or Laughton's, but far less productive. They had fished hard for a week without a sign of a tunny, but on the final day, they set off before first light with the groundless optimism all anglers know well.

By noon, they had found a trawler and, to their surprise, it reported plenty of tunny were about. As the haul began, Taylor threw his baited herring overboard and in fully half a minute found himself attached to a fish. Sadly, the cod-end of the trawler's net was still in the water and within seconds the tunny had used it to make good its escape. Before long, Taylor had retrieved his trace, rebaited and hooked another fish, which managed to throw the hook after a run of no more than twenty yards. The third fish managed a much longer run before snapping the line, while the fourth and fifth fish came and went without the hapless Taylor knowing quite what had happened.

He had been fishing for just ten minutes and lost five fish, but tunny were still about and a sixth was soon hooked. This was undoubtedly a big fish, 'in the neighbourhood of 700lb', Taylor ruefully recalled, and this time, it managed to avoid the still hauling trawler. After quarter of an hour, with Taylor beginning to think he might just break his run of bad luck, the hook pulled free.

Before Taylor could cast again, however, the trawler had shot her net and fishing was out of the question. Not one to take defeat lying down, he waited the three hours until it hauled again. When it finally began to haul, Taylor managed to lose three more fish in quick succession - one of them when his line tangled with one of the six other anglers who had appeared in that small patch of the North Sea. At one point, three anglers were into tunny at the same time, but while the other two landed their fish - in both cases, their first - the experienced Taylor somehow didn't. By the end of the second haul, he had lost eleven tunny that day, and it was with an air of desperation that he hastily arranged a 'private haul' with the skipper of the trawler. Alas, the North Sea now seemed empty of tunny and he made for home a dazed, fishless soul.

Tom Pashby silently handed him a bottle of beer and they drowned their sorrows. Taylor was by nature a stoic character - he dismissed sea sickness, for example, as 'largely a matter of nerves' - but as they arrived back at Scarborough, even he insisted his boatman 'put that darned flag at half mast'.

Eleven lost fish after seven blank days may seem extraordinarily bad luck, but in tunny fishing, there would always be somebody with a sorrier tale to tell. Lorenzo Mitchell-Henry cites the story of the unlucky - and sadly unknown - angler who played a fish for nineteen hours, getting towed some 120 miles in the process, only to lose it. 'It is a maddening game,' reflected Taylor. 'A stupid game. No regular hours for sleep; no regular hours for food; verily, a silly game. A snare and a delusion . . . and if you asked me, "Is it worth all this trouble?" I would say, most emphatically, "Yes." It is glorious madness, glorious folly - and when the long day closes and you have been fortunate enough to land your first fish, I hope I may be one of those to shake you by the hand.'

7

A Boy's Story

*I am still young enough to be thrilled to the core
each time I go after these wonderful fish*

Smiling shyly, John Holdsworth gazes at the camera. It is 1934 and, like many visitors that year, John is in Scarborough to catch himself a tunny. He is not, however, a battle-hardened veteran of big game fishing. Nor, for that matter, is he one of the bright young things keen to combine some tunny fishing with Scarborough's new social whirl. John Holdsworth is a fourteen-year-old schoolboy, on holiday from Harrow School.

John Holdsworth in 1934.

The Pennine.

John was born in 1920, the eldest son of George Bertram Holdsworth and his wife, Mabel. George is now the head of Holdsworths, a leading light in Halifax's textiles industry, and has used this success to fund an enthusiastic pursuit of country sports, including shooting, hunting and deep sea fishing, and travel to destinations as diverse as Switzerland, Australia, New Zealand, Rhodesia and the Canary Islands. Described in 1913 as 'one of the best speakers that the (Conservative) party possesses amongst the younger politicians in the county borough', he has been a champion of tariff reform, an opponent of National Insurance and has used his position to take 'a real interest in the uplifting of the working man'.

In 1932, however, while grouse shooting on Coniston Moor with friends, George received tragic news. His wife, Mabel, had succumbed to her cancer far sooner than anyone expected. It was a loss from which George never really recovered. He did remarry, in 1936, but the relationship soon broke down irretrievably. George was again grouse shooting when his second wife arranged a removal van to seize many of their home's contents. An astonished butler despatched a servant to run up to the moor, but George's response showed an admirable sense of priorities. When told his wife was effectively robbing him, he reportedly replied "Let her! I'm shooting!"

It should be no surprise, perhaps, that his fourteen-year-old son was prepared to try for a giant tunny far out in the North Sea. John's photographs from 1934 are the snapshots of a schoolboy on some marvellous adventure. He enthusiastically photographed Scarborough's harbour and some drifters setting sail before following them to sea in the *Prospecto*. Details of the trip are scarce, but it is known that they followed the drifters out to the Dogger Bank, some 110 miles from Scarborough. There they waited while the herring fleet, among them *The Pennine*, hauled their nets. At some point on 6th September, the young angler hooked his tunny . . .

When John Holdsworth's tunny was brought ashore, having

The tunny safely stowed on deck.

travelled back to Scarborough lashed to the deck of their boat, it weighed 614lb. It earned him a Class IV Grey Seal Certificate from the British Tunny Club, proof that it was beaten unaided on line of less than 180lb breaking strain, and gave its captor a fleeting moment of fame in *The Times*, which noted that the fish had completely swallowed the hook and was defeated after a 'short fight'.

For all Mitchell-Henry's carping about the fighting powers of 'soft fish' from the Dogger Bank, it was a remarkable feat for such a young boy. The crowds of people looking on as John Holdsworth posed with his fish would certainly have thought so, particularly the local children who would gather whenever a tunny was brought ashore. F. B. Hannam was once moved to describe the shrill cries he faced each time he came into port, tunny pennant flying, adding that 'whatever Yorkshire children cannot do, there is one thing in which they can beat the world, and that is yell!'

John and his 614lb fish on the quay at Scarborough.

The Prospecto *flies the Tunny Club flag denoting a landed fish.*

As the eldest son, John Holdsworth was being groomed to take over the family business, and there is no record of him returning to fish at Scarborough. On 3rd July, 1939, Harrow's school certificate register records that 'Mr John started work', but exactly one month later, war broke out. John had already joined the Territorial Army earlier that year and was soon commissioned into the King's Royal Rifle Corps. He fought in North Africa at the height of the campaign against Rommel, and was awarded the Military Cross while serving with the Eighth Army.

In July 1942, three weeks before El Alamein, John suffered multiple shrapnel wounds and was evacuated to England, but after convalescing, he returned to serve in North-Western Europe. It was here in 1945, with an Allied victory in sight, that Major John Holdsworth MC was fatally wounded, a week before his twenty-fifth birthday. His younger brother, William, wrote a month later that he had heard John 'put up a wonderful show just before he fell'.

John Holdsworth's name is inscribed in the Harrow School War Memorial, and the larger window at Saint Mary's Church, Kettlewell, is dedicated to his memory. Holdsworths, the family firm which he had been groomed to take over, still prospers, as it has done since 1822. Few details are left of a life that, like so many of his contemporaries, was cruelly cut short. But thanks to the recent work of his nephew, David Holdsworth, John's holiday photographs survive. And over seventy years later, we can still see Scarborough's tunny years through the eyes of an excited, wide-eyed, fourteen-year-old boy . . .

8

A Sporting Chance

For nearly an hour the battle rages with the
pounding exhaustion of a steeplechase,
puny man and giant mackerel.

Fish are revered for many reasons, but never more than for their fighting power. A double figure bream, for example, is arguably harder to come by than a barbel of the same weight, yet legends don't abound of battles with these slab-sided cyprinids. A big bream is theoretically impressive, of course, but a monster barbel is viscerally so. Anthropomorphic anglers may like to bestow cunning and intelligence on their quarry, but we prefer it when they also pull back a bit. It certainly sounds better in the lounge bar.

The tunny, then, was surely the acme of British angling. The modern angler now has to travel abroad to experience anything like the size or power of *Thunnus thynnus*, and enjoys the advantages of modern rods, hugely engineered reels and sport fishing boats able to reverse after a hooked fish. In Scarborough's tunny years, the rod was of split cane or hickory. It was a staggeringly cumbersome weapon and carried a reel as heavy as a small child. How on earth must it have felt being tethered to 800lb of irate fish, wielding such antediluvian tackle?

Unsurprisingly, tunny literature is replete with fighting hyperbole. David Carl Forbes, for example, claimed that 'the tunny is probably the only fish in British waters, with the possible exception of a really huge halibut, capable of stripping most of the line from a reel . . . It is for good reason that tunny have the big-game reputation of fighting their heart out to the death.'

Indeed they did. More than once, tunny hastened their demise by plummeting to the seabed and expiring on impact, leaving the angler with the onerous task of dragging a considerable dead weight back to the surface. 'In a good many cases,' commented the ever-pithy Fred Taylor, 'he gives up the ghost and plunges to the bottom stone dead, from whence one has to try and get him up by the pleasant little form of exercise known as 'pumping'. It is a thoroughly exhausting business, but has to be done.'

The tunny's fighting characteristics were quite unlike most pelagic game fish. In contrast to billfish, for example, they did not spend most of the battle airborne, something Mitchell-Henry felt posed more of a challenge to the angler: 'It does not dissipate its resources by spectacular gymnastics . . . the whole of its strength is thus expended in direct conflict with the angler.'

Fred Taylor, however, disagreed. 'There is one thing I rather regret when you are fighting a tunny . . . he does not jump out of the water.'

Either way, there can be no doubt that a hooked tunny was a serious proposition, even if it usually remained beneath the waves until its final moments. But the tunny, it should be said, was not the only big fish in British waters. More than one shark was taken by Tunny Club members off Scarborough, and the blues, porbeagle and occasional threshers caught off our coast were the tunny's obvious heavyweight rivals. Eric Horsfall Turner, however, felt there was nothing to compare with a tunny. 'Comparison between (a shark's) fighting power and that of a tunny,' he observed, 'is like comparing the fight of a 14lb sack of potatoes and a salmon of the same weight.'

Harold J. Hardy was one of the most prominent ambassadors for *Thunnus thynnus*. He regularly expounded on the tunny's fighting qualities in books and magazines, with his chapter for *Angling* (1936), detailing the fight with a 630lb specimen, being one of his more evocative efforts:

There is a terrific pull which almost wrenches the angler from his seat, and we are into a tunny. Instantly it shoots straight under the trawler, our boatman pulls round its bows and we give the fish line and luckily come clear. Two hundred and fifty yards of line have left the reel already and the tunny is careering madly, towing us along at some five miles an hour. If we are to make a quick fight of it and kill the fish, this is the time to commence the battle. If we don't, it will possibly take hours, and, even then, as our strength gives out, the fish may escape.

At last! Here he comes . . . We see the gleaming side of the fish within twenty yards, a sure sign that he has had enough. Another supreme effort of pumping as the trace breaks the surface . . . The gaff is plunged home in the fish and a turn taken with the rope attached to the gaff head round some suitable anchorage. We admire its beautiful streamlined form, built for speed. The colouring is magnificent, but unfortunately it soon fades.

The tunny's fighting power was obviously eulogised in the angling press, at least in the early years, but the fish's reputation soon reached a wider audience. *The Times*, for example, ran several articles on tunny fishing in the Thirties, including a vivid depiction by E. T. Peel in September 1932:

Owing to the splendid fighting qualities of the tunny, and the fact that he is caught on comparatively light tackle from a small boat in the open sea, the new sport affords more excitement than any other form of angling, and tests the skill, strength, and endurance of the angler to the utmost. Moreover, the fish can be seen in action, on the surface and under, as they break water continuously while feeding, throwing themselves partly out of the sea in wild dashes to take the bait. While feeding on the surface or in a state of excitement the tunny erect the great anterior dorsal fin, which is otherwise carried in a slot sunk completely in the back. It shows invariably when the fish breaks water, but does not appear to be used under water, though doubtless brought into action at times to preserve balance. His speed and power are tremendous; so great is the pressure on the line that it becomes necessary to release the reel brake to avoid a smash. In his first great effort to escape, the fish takes complete command, and the angler can only hope that hook and tackle will hold. After his first run the tunny usually works to the surface, swimming strongly and steadily with the boat in tow at three to four knots, a speed which he can, if allowed, keep up for hours on end. But no respite should be given. Every foot of line must be stubbornly contested, and every ruse in playing tried to keep the fish moving, so that he expends his strength before the angler tires. Attempts to sound must be resisted . . . every limb and muscle being brought into play in a sustained effort to hold the fish near the surface. Seamanship and quick, skilful handling of the boat, calling for considerable experience, are important factors in playing the fish. And so the desperate struggle continues, each move of the fish being countered until, exhausted or dead, he is brought to the gaff.

This was stirring stuff, but proved too strong for the stomachs of some readers. Sir Henry Hesketh Joudou Bell (*sic*), a tireless author, diarist and former governor of improbably-named colonial outposts, was moved to write a lengthy response to *The Times'* editor:

Sir, The writer graphically described the 'splendid fighting qualities' of the fish; how, after being hooked, it rushes off at terrific speed, plunges to great depths, and 'for hours' may tow a boat at a speed of three or four knots. He said that every foot of line must be stubbornly contested to keep the fish going, each move of the fish being countered until, 'exhausted or dead', it is brought to the surface. This was described as the new 'grand sport'. Maybe, but what of the fish? Surely the essence of 'sport' is to secure your quarry with a minimum of suffering to the victim. In this case the

*unfortunate creature is killed not by a sudden blow or shot, but by a tor-
turing struggle that may last for hours. One may dwell on the excitement
of the fisherman, sitting in his 14ft. boat . . . tugging for hours at his
line, but is that really 'sport?' What would we think of the man who,
instead of killing a stag with a single, unerring shot, contrived, if such a
thing were possible, to project a large hook into the nostrils of the animal
and then proceed to 'play' it for hours until the tortured creature, worn
and harried to death by its frantic rushes, leaps, and struggles, expired
from sheer exhaustion and terror?*

Fortunately, tunny fishing had Lorenzo Mitchell-Henry on its
side. Not a man to suffer fools, whether gladly or otherwise,
his response was uncharacteristically restrained, but nevertheless
did a good job defending the sport he had created:

*Sir, Is it possible that Sir Hesketh Bell is serious when he suggests . . . that
tunny fishing is cruel? The tunny is of enormous power, and while per-
sonally I have fought well over a hundred of them I have succeeded in
bringing only 10 to the gaff. The '4in. steel hook' and the '12ft. steel
trace' referred to by your correspondent are no more formidable, in pro-
portion, than the gossamer threads and tiny hooks used in dryfly fishing.
In fact it has always surprised onlookers that such a huge and powerful
fish of sometimes over 10ft. in length and 7ft. in girth, weighing almost
800 1b., could be subdued on such light tackle. Your correspondent's sug-
gestion of 'playing a stag' is interesting, and I think that if the animal was
to be given the choice of the certain freedom from the rod and line or the
certain death or wounds from being shot unawares from a few paces, it
would choose the former. Since Sir Hesketh Bell writes from Gibraltar,
perhaps he would be kind enough to acquaint himself with the prospects
of tunny fishing in those parts and let people know, for they are to be
found in large numbers off Cadiz and Huelva in the months from June
to October.*

Sir Hesketh wisely avoided a war of words with Mitchell-Henry,
and tunny fishing continued to be celebrated as one of the

pinnacles of angling endeavour, at least for the time being.

Whether despite or because of the tunny's much-publicised fighting power, considerable thought was given to appropriately sporting tackle with which to battle them. The early pioneers were not about to use overly-heavy tackle, even for such huge fish. When the British Tunny Club assumed control of the sport in 1933, it gave greater merit to captures made on comparatively lighter tackle. Initially, Blue, Orange and Grey Seals were awarded for tunny landed on lines of 100lb, 130lb and 160lb dry breaking strain, although this was later amended to include a highly coveted Green Button for fish of over 200lb caught on line of up to 80lb b.s. The length of line allowed was unlimited - a moot point given the relatively limited capacity of reels at the time - but with a trace not exceeding twenty feet.

Similarly, the Club said rods should be 'in accordance with sporting ethics and customs', although it did not expand on this notion and admitted that a 'certain latitude is allowed'. More specifically, anglers must hook, fight and bring their fish to gaff unaided, without resting the rod on the gunwale of the boat or resorting to hand-lining, shooting or harpoons. In short, then, tunny should be caught on tackle and using methods that gave the fish as much of a fighting chance as the angler.

So was the tunny the pinnacle of angling achievement; the toughest challenge an ambitious big game fisherman could face? Perhaps not. 'One of the least exciting fish I remember weighed nearly 500lb,' recalled Horsfall Turner. 'It was a firmly-hooked bluefin tunny which came alongside, played out hard, after a 15 minute fight on a tranquil and unobstructed North Sea.'

Horsfall Turner's fish may have been unusual, but it was not the only one to admit defeat sooner than might be expected. In the sport's early years, battles with even modest-sized tunny frequently lasted several hours, but as the years passed, the time spent to subdue tunny seemed to fall steadily. Mitchell-Henry, an early champion of the tunny's fighting powers, appeared to have altered his opinion by the mid Thirties. 'One gallant

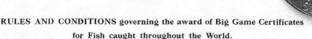

THE BRITISH TUNNY CLUB

RULES AND CONDITIONS governing the award of Big Game Certificates

for Fish caught throughout the World.

(Minimum weight one hundred pounds)

CERTIFICATES bearing the Seal of the Club will be issued for Tunny and other fish caught on line having maximum dry breaking strains as follows :—

Class I.	BLUE SEAL Maximum dry b/s.			100 lb.
Class II.	ORANGE SEAL	,,	,, ,,	130 lb.
Class III.	GREY SEAL	,,	,, ,,	160 lb.

A DECLARATION must be made on the form provided by the Club and forwarded to the secretaries within ONE MONTH of the capture of the fish together with a registration fee of 2/6.

TACKLE SPECIFICATIONS. Rod length shall not be less than 6 ft. 6 ins. overall, consisting of top and butt ; the top shall not weigh more than 44 oz. and be not less than 4 ft. 6 ins. in length. Length of line shall be unlimited and the last 20 ft. may be doubled.

TRACE shall not exceed 20 feet.

FISHING RULES.

1. THE FISH must be played and brought to the gaff (or in the case of Sharks the Harpoon) by the angler unaided, using tackle conforming to the above specification.

2. NO HANDLINING shall be allowed.

3. No floats causing an appreciable drag on the fish shall be allowed.

4. Neither the rod, reel, line nor any part of the equipment worn may be secured to the boat, but a loose safety line may be used which will in no way serve as an aid in playing the fish.

5. The trace shall not be handled except for the purpose of gaffing the fish.

6. A fish shall not be gaffed from a boat other than the one in which the angler is at the time of gaffing.

7. The fish must be weighed in the presence of an official appointed or recognised by the Committee except when a fish is landed at a place where there is no official weigher, in which case the Committee must be satisfied that these rules have been complied with and the weight properly ascertained.

8. Members shall fish only with rod and line and permit fishing by their crew only under the rules of the Club, except for special scientific research and then only with the sanction of the Committee.

9. The decision of the Committee with regard to the interpretation of these rules or with regard to any point arising thereunder shall be final.

Club rules 1934.

angler,' he recalled, 'who has consistently lost these fighting fish and whose fights, and blisters, have become historic for more than one reason, captured five fish in less than one hour's actual time.'

Similarly, Fred Taylor, who enjoyed several epic battles in his time and who advised would-be tunny anglers to play fish hard

THE BRITISH TUNNY CLUB.

RULES AND CONDITIONS
governing the granting of Certificates for Fish caught throughout the World.

CLUB BUTTONS will be issued for Tunny and other fish certified as caught on line having maximum dry breaking strains as follows :—

Class 1.	GREEN BUTTON	Maximum dry b/s.		80 lb.
Class II.	BLUE BUTTON	Maximum	,, ,,	100 lb.
Class III.	ORANGE BUTTON	Maximum	,, ,,	130 lb.
Class IV.	GREY BUTTON	Maximum	,, ,,	160 lb.

Classes II, III and IV, Buttons will only be awarded for fish of over 200 lb. Only one button in each class will be awarded to any one member, *i.e.*, four buttons in all.

All certified fish will be registered in the Club Register. Certificates bearing seals green, blue, orange or grey according to their class, will be awarded on application.

A DECLARATION must be made on the form provided by the Club and forwarded to the secretaries within TWENTY-FOUR HOURS of the capture of the fish together with a registration fee of 2/6.

TACKLE SPECIFICATIONS. Rod length shall not be less than 6 ft. 6 ins. overall, consisting of tip and butt ; the tip shall not weigh more than 44 oz. and be not less than 4 ft. 6 ins. in length. Length of line shall be unlimited and the last 20 ft. may be doubled.

TRACE shall not exceed 20 feet.

FISHING RULES.

1. THE FISH must be played and brought to the gaff (or in case of Sharks, the Harpoon) by the angler unaided using rod and line only, and on tackle conforming to the above specifications.

2. NO HANDLINING shall be allowed.

3. No floats causing an appreciable drag on the fish shall be allowed.

4. Neither the reel, line nor any part of the equipment worn may be secured to the boat, but the rod may be attached to the butt socket by means of a pin or other device and a loose safety line may be used which will in no way serve as an aid in playing the fish.

5. The trace shall not be handled except for the purpose of gaffing the fish.

6. A fish shall not be gaffed from a boat other than the one in which the angler is at the time of gaffing.

7. The fish must be weighed in the presence of an official appointed or recognised by the Committee except when a fish is landed at a place where there is no official weigher, in which case the Committee must be satisfied that these rules have been complied with and the weight properly ascertained.

8. The decision of the Committee with regard to the interpretation of these rules or with regard to any point arising thereunder shall be final.

NOTE—For the guidance of new members. The Committee will consider as an unsporting act, the resting of the rod on the gunwale or any other part of the boat for the purpose of taking a rest while playing a fish. Such action will disqualify the offender from receiving a certificate.

4

Club rules 1949.

'if you can stand the strain', saw something of a change as more and more were caught. 'I had reckoned that the average time for catching these fish,' he mused, 'was, roughly, half an hour per 100lb; but this year . . . many of the fish were killed in an incredibly short time. For instance, the 798lb world-record fish was captured in 48 minutes.'

Not surprisingly, the erratic fighting quality of North Sea tunny provoked a debate in the angling press and, even less surprisingly, Lorenzo Mitchell-Henry was at the centre of it all. As early as 1932, he was raising the issue, and one or two of his colleagues' hackles. 'The experiences of Col. Peel,' he wrote, 'who is an old hand at big fish angling but a beginner at tunny fishing, are of much interest to me as an old hand at the game. I have, I may say without fear of challenge, by far the most powerful tackle ever produced for encountering these fish, and when I heard of Col. Peel and other novices landing 700-pounders in less than an hour . . . I began to think something radically wrong with my methods.'

Mitchell-Henry, of course, thought no such thing. He was not, after all, a man given to public bouts of self-doubt. The reason for such early capitulation, he suggested, was that they were recently spawned female fish. Would the fishery scientists, he asked, in between a barrage of statistics about the time taken to subdue various tunny, like to confirm exactly when and where tunny breeding took place?

Fred Taylor was the first angler to respond in print. He agreed that breeding habits may have an influence on a tunny's fighting spirit, but added that the 'all out from the word go' approach, pioneered by Col. Peel, was perhaps the deciding factor. His letter also corrected a number of statements made by Mitchell-Henry, setting the tone for a wonderfully tetchy series of letters, even by tunny fishing standards. Taylor may have been one of the scene's more affable characters, but even he could be pedantic when provoked. His 735lb fish of 1930, he said, took not four hours to land, as Mitchell-Henry had claimed, but three hours and thirty-five minutes. Similarly, his tackle was not the same as he had always used, but now included a rather heavier rod. Furthermore, his recent 707lb tunny was landed not in 'a little over an hour', as stated, but took almost two and a half.

On the same page, Mitchell-Henry was now fermenting a

frank exchange of views with Col. Stapleton-Cotton, who had attributed to him the phrase *so-called novices.* 'I resent Colonel Cotton's phrase,' said Mitchell-Henry. 'If Colonel Cotton would at least try to give us some information instead of always "picking" on me and my tackle, he would serve a more useful purpose in the advancement of this sport inaugurated by me.' He then ridiculed a claim by Stapleton-Cotton that his tackle could lift 80lb. 'Did he lift 80lb with his rod and reel *under fishing conditions?*' And if he did so, did he use the harness of my design which he got from me some years ago, or the harness that was 'smashed to bits' *vide* Col. Peel's letter to *The Times?*'

Rising to his theme, Mitchell-Henry then repeated a challenge he had already made in *The Field*: 'I will deposit £25 with you, sir, if Col. Cotton will deposit a similar amount, and I will give a demonstration of my tackle and five-year-old reel on which I have landed seven tunny under fishing conditions, he to do the same, but to use the tackle he has just tested, but not to use any part of it designed by me, the loser's £25 to go to a charity chosen by the winner. To use an Americanism, he can now *pay up or shut up.*'

Stapleton-Cotton's reply was admirably restrained. 'I was very pained to read Mr Mitchell-Henry's explosive letter . . . and to think that I had offended him. His tackle must indeed be remarkable . . . I certainly would not dare compete. The outfit I tested will hold a pull of over 80 pounds at a fishing angle, and is eminently successful at killing big game fish. [It] would not lift 80lb under any conditions, though it would hold that pull. I have one of his harnesses, but I do not use it as I prefer a rope one. I have not yet found a really satisfactory harness, they are all rather apt to ruck up on one's neck.'

Mitchell-Henry, meanwhile, had turned his attention to Fred Taylor, whose temerity in correcting him could not go unremarked. His letter was disarmingly pleasant at first, thanking Taylor profusely for correcting the earlier errors, although he felt it was rather like 'splitting hairs'. Pleasantries over, Mitchell-

Henry then went on the offensive. 'Would Mr Taylor give me his assurance that he was able . . . to land his fish this year without having to resort to hand lining? In 1930 we were all as disappointed as he was that as his tackle was unable to raise his fish he had been obliged to allow it to be hand lined, and for that reason could not claim the Blue Ribbon of angling, viz. the certificate of the BSAS.'

Taylor's advice to play fish hard was also ridiculed. 'He certainly went "all out" on his fish in 1930,' recalled Mitchell-Henry, 'and was "all in" when Mr Hannam and I got to him and put his fish aboard for him!' Despite this, he also claimed that he himself had never done anything other than play his fish as hard as possible, as 'a ton and a half of fish in seven hours somewhat points to'.

Given such damning ripostes, newcomers to tunny fishing could be forgiven for passing up the chance to take on the sport's founding father in print. Captain C. H. Frisby, however, did just that. 'As one of the novices who has yet to catch his first fish,' he wrote, little knowing just how successful a tunny angler he would soon become, 'I hesitate to enter the lists to tilt with such an experienced wielder of rod and pen as Mr Mitchell-Henry, but on one point I must, to alter the metaphor, cross swords with him . . . the length of time required to bring the fish to the gaff must, to a very large extent, depend on the skill and methods employed by the fisherman.'

This was a brave opening gambit from an angler still to bring a tunny to the gaff himself, but stronger stuff was to follow. 'Mr Mitchell-Henry, in his letter to you . . . ends with these words: 'It would be unwise to limit the strength of lines . . . or any part of the tackle.' Now, sir, is this tunny fishing in the North Sea to be a sport or a commercial business? In my opinion, to use a line of unlimited strength . . . seems to be on a par with going after a tiger in a whippet tank or deer stalking with a machine gun. What fun can there be had in hooking a fish and knowing that he cannot break you?'

The debate continued well into the 1933 season and may well have hastened the setting up of the British Tunny Club. Whatever the reasons for 'hard' and 'soft' tunny, as they were known, there was obviously a need for new rules to govern sporting methods. The club's recently-anointed president, Colonel Peel, explained that line strength should be limited to 54 strand - with 72 strand for the 1933 season only - in order to 'check the tendency of a mere "heave and haul" process on super-strong line replacing the skill in rod play and tactics that is called for on lighter'. The aim was not to discourage those who wished to catch tunny on their own terms, he said, but to enforce 'competitive' terms under which trophies and certificates could be awarded.

The *Fishing Gazette*, however, had its own views. 'We doubt if a 1,000lb tunny could be landed under the existing rules,' it said, 'unless it happened to be suffering from an inferiority complex. As an alternative to the restriction on the strength of lines, we would suggest restricting the strength of the hook, or, better still, limiting the line capacity of the reel and allowing any line size.'

During the 1933 season, however, a new debate was stirring. Talk was less of suitable tackle and more of the sort of vessels used by new tunny anglers. Motor boats had now become a regular feature for Scarborough's tunny anglers. Yes, the keel boats and cobles used to tow row boats to the grounds were motorised, but hitherto the actual fishing had always been done from a small boat powered by nothing more than determination and Yorkshire grit. Mitchell-Henry was not alone in feeling that this was not just the best way, but the only way to go about the business of sport fishing. 'I have always been opposed to the use of power and machinery for sport,' he declared, 'such as motor boats for fishing, motor cars for lion and other big game hunting, and aeroplanes for duck shooting; but I have no objection to these sportsmen using tanks for fox hunting.'

'From the moment this fishing is allowed to be done from motor boats,' he argued, more seriously, 'it should be understood that but little skill is required to get fish . . . the necessity for rules fades away and the whole sport dissolves itself into an ambition to "get" the largest fish.'

Even when traditional row boats were used, however, the increased range of the vessels used to tow them to sea had an influence. Dogger Bank was undoubtedly a feeding ground for a much higher concentration of tunny than were found closer to port. It was the Dogger Bank fish, argued Mitchell-Henry, that were prone to succumbing rather easily, 'soft' fish that were out of condition and incapable of putting up a decent account of themselves. 'No living creature is capable of great exertion when replete with food,' he explained. 'It would look as if the fish on the Dogger Bank are nearly all of the soft type . . . a large number of soft or weak fish, which were captured with remarkable ease far out to sea.'

When tunny fishing was carried out away from the Dogger Bank, said Mitchell-Henry, some fifteen to twenty miles off-shore, for example, their fighting abilities were much more impressive. He also felt that the methods used to hook a tunny could dictate how it fought. In particular, he was bitterly opposed to the late striking, and subsequent deep hooking, used by some anglers. 'When a fish takes the bait it should be struck at once,' he declared. 'By letting a fish have slack line on its taking a bait, and waiting before striking, the hook may not be struck home until it has been swallowed.' Not only was this likely to prove fatal to any lost fish, he stated, but no tunny was likely to give of its best with a hook deep in its throat.

The fighting quality of tunny was a theme Mitchell-Henry returned to again and again. As late as March 1949, he wrote to his favourite sounding board, the *Fishing Gazette*, airing his views: 'It has been clearly shown that the fighting qualities of tunny taken on rod and line vary considerably. The behaviour of those sought on their feeding grounds, such as the Dogger Bank or round the herring drifters at night, cannot be compared with the terrific fights that certain well-known anglers, such as Ross, Zane Grey, Mitchell and others, have had with these fish in good condition.'

'Further instances are shown by the capture of these fish by young girls in half an hour, and catches of up to seven fish in a single day by one angler,' he wrote. 'Lone fish hooked in day-light put up the greatest sporting fights, as also do those hooked around the trawlers, since, when following the trawlers for many hours, they do not get much food beyond that which is stirred up by the trawl when travelling, or those thrown to them by the crews . . . these fish usually put up great fights, but here

*Mr Gifford off
Scarborough
in 1934.*

*Below: A keel boat
returns to harbour
in 1952.*

M.

Brookfield,
141, Fairfax Road,
Teddington, Middx.

6th December, 1951.

Dear Taylor,

With reference to the questionnaire, concerning the qualification of Mr. Wasdell's fish, and the opinions I expressed at the meeting on 30th November, I would confirm that my interpretation of the rules is that, because it was not caught from a row-boat, it does not qualify for a certificate.

In my opinion, there is sufficient supporting evidence to confirm that, by force of custom, for a fish to qualify, it must be caught from a row-boat, and I am confident that the conclusions of a fully attended meeting of the Committee would endorse this.

In the years 1930, 1931 and 1932, the certificates issued were classed as rowing-boat certificates.

In the year 1933, the value of the certificate was split up in relation to the weight of the fish.

In the year 1934, there was an additional split in relation to the strength of the line used.

As far as I am aware, at no time have the rules changed on the basic point at issue.

Moreover, from articles in the Press, talks on the B.B.C., at all meetings and discussions, and even in the illustrations on the covers of our Bulletin, the belief, both nationally and internationally, is that the rules of the British Tunny Club are based upon fishing for tunny from row-boat. Even as recently as 1950, when the world's record of 977 lbs. was registered, the successful fisherman proudly made it known that he had caught his fish according to British Tunny Club rules, in particular from an open row-boat.

Tunny Club politics.

-2-

Furthermore, if this were not the understanding of all members, why, when new members (including Wasdell) are being briefed, do we tell them they must have a row-boat? Why do we go to all measures to secure row-boats, and why does the President specifically state, in his letter in the 1951 Bulletin, when quoting the cost of hiring, "plus cost of row-boat and boatman" in each case, if the use of a row-boat is not a rule, by force of custom?

There are many other such points which can be cited to confirm that at no time has there been any other thought in anybody's mind but that a row-boat must be used, and for goodness' sake let us apply the rules as they have been followed since the Club was formed.

The next thing we shall hear is that someone has caught a fish from a helicopter, and, because this is not specifically mentioned in the rules, it will qualify. Don't let us give people like M.W. another opportunity to raise a storm, on the strength of saying we stretch the rules to suit a particular case.

Sincerely,

H. E. Weatherley.

F. Taylor Esq.,
Stonefield,
Lynchmere,
Nr. Haslemere,
Surrey.

Copy to F. Watkinson Esq.

[136]

again much depends on the location of the hook. If hooked in the throat, or deep down in the gullet, oesophagorrhagia may ensue, causing almost total collapse.'

Ironically, his letter sat next to the story of a 28lb pike caught in a Walthamstow reservoir, which took well over two hours to land - far longer than many tunny over twenty times its weight.

The issue of how to properly fight a tunny continued to vex Mitchell-Henry, and later that year, as the 1949 tunny season drew to a close, he again wrote to the *Fishing Gazette*. His letter, headlined 'Is Tunny Fishing Sport?' argued that 'it certainly is and can be, if done under the rules of the British Sea Anglers Society'. For once, he avoided any direct attack on the British Tunny Club, although his inference was clear, but he did aim a more explicit barb at his American counterparts: 'it is difficult to understand how hauling in the line - with a fish on the end of it - with a heavily gloved left hand and reeling in the slack with the right hand, as shown, described and practised by big-game fishermen in the States, is not bare-faced hand-lining.'

Once again, Mitchell-Henry finished his missive with a plea for simple row boats and early striking, although by this time, he had long since ceased to be a part of Scarborough's annual tunny hunt himself. Whether this was because tunny were no longer the battlers of old, or because he now had a rather jaundiced view of the tunny scene and its social shenanigans, is highly debatable. Certainly, some tunny may have given their captors a rather easier time of it than others, but even Mitchell-Henry conceded that on their day, and under the right circumstances, a fit tunny was worth its fearsome reputation. With those that didn't, he argued, it was usually the anglers, and not the fish, that were at fault.

9

Sandgate Society

Tunny? I've seen something about them in the papers.
Big things, aren't they?

'Among comparatively wealthy sportsmen, thought not neces-sarily anglers, it soon became fashionable to spend a week or fortnight with the tunny fleet.' So wrote Eric Horsfall Turner in Jack Thorndike's *Sea Fishing with the Experts*, in a typical broad-side at some of the nouveau types who turned up, aboard increasingly ostentatious yachts, during August and September. Horsfall Turner was not impressed. 'The average run of those who brought their lovely sea craft to Scarborough South Bay,' he opined, 'are mainly interested in an amusing party and the ego-satisfying asset of having caught so big a fish.'

His view wasn't entirely unfounded. Public figures seemed drawn to tunny fishing. Sir Miles Lampson, for example, who managed a brace of tunny in 1935, was a British Ambassador to Egypt. Captain T. L. Dugdale, who took a fish of 638lb in 1933, later became Minister for Agriculture. So many anglers were making their way up from London that LNER advertised a special rail service to Scarborough, with a Frank Mason poster that was more redolent of the French Riviera than it was of a wet and windy North Sea.

Many of Scarborough's visitors were little-known in less

Below: August 1933. Amongst the tunny fishers at Dogger Bank are Lord Moyne and Lady Broughton.
(Photo by Topical Press Agency/Getty Images)

glamorous angling circles, a fact more than one writer chose to hold against them. But to dismiss them as a bunch of idle rich thrill-seekers, as some did, is misleading. Many of these rich sports were noted big game anglers, not to mention highly successful in other areas of life. In terms of military or industrial success, for example, the British Tunny Club was surely one of the most distinguished sporting groups of all time.

In a club replete with splendidly-monikered military heroes, however, Captain C. H. Frisby VC stood out. Cyril Hubert Frisby was born in Barnet in September 1885, and enlisted with the Hampshire Regiment as a Private in 1916. The following year he was commissioned into the Coldstream Guards First Battalion, with whom he went on to earn the British War Medal, Victory Medal and Victoria Cross. His VC was awarded for what the *London Gazette* termed 'conspicuous bravery, leadership and devotion to duty' alongside Pte T. N. Jackson at the Canal Du Nord in September 1918.

The then Lieutenant (Acting Captain) Frisby was leading a company detailed to recapture a canal crossing on the Demicourt-Graincourt Road, when he and his men came under 'annihilating' machine gun fire from a post under the bridge. They were unable to advance, despite reinforcements, and Frisby realised that the whole operation in the area would fail unless the crossing was secured. Calling for volunteers to follow him, he dashed forward and climbed into the canal, under heavy machine gun fire from point blank range, and secured the machine gun post despite a bayonet wound to the leg. This first objective achieved, he was then able to reorganise the defences of another company on his right, which had lost all its officers, while repelling a hostile counter attack. Despite his injury, he remained at his post throughout, showing 'a fine example to all ranks'.

In 1920, he resigned his commission and worked at the Stock Exchange, a career which some years later would give him the means to enjoy all that Scarborough had to offer. But Frisby's wealth and military record should not obscure the fact that he was also an astonishingly successful tunny angler. He landed fifteen certified tunny in just two years, including an astonishing haul of five fish, for a combined world record weight of 2,812lb, in just one day. If Frisby had just been interested in the 'ego-satisfying asset of . . . so big a fish', why then did he keep returning to Scarborough, at considerable expense, after his record catch?

Frisby was not a particularly flamboyant figure, but tunny fishing did attract its share. Even among the tunny fraternity's ritzier characters, however, Lord Moyne cut a singular dash in his red flannel suit. Moyne was born Walter Edward Guinness in Dublin, 1880, the third son of the 1st Earl of Iveagh. After Eton, he served in the South African War, where he was wounded and mentioned in despatches. Guinness was then elected as the Conservative MP for Bury St Edmunds, although the First World War again saw him in action, this time with the Suffolk Yeomanry, in Egypt and at Gallipoli. He was later appointed Under Secretary for War, the first of a number of roles which eventually saw him serve as Minister for Agriculture.

In 1929, he retired from office and became Baron Moyne of Bury St Edmunds, a role that allowed him to indulge his love of travel, exploration and tunny high society. With the outbreak of a second world war, however, he returned to politics, eventually becoming, in January 1944, Minister Resident in the Middle East. The British Foreign Office was then considered pro-Arab, and within ten months, Moyne was assassinated by Zionist groups under the control of future Israeli President, Yitzhak Shamir. Without Moyne's presence, British politics and the post-war tunny community were decidedly less colourful.

That said, the British Tunny Club was never short of politicians or military types, and in Brigadier Sir Otho Leslie Prior-Palmer DSO, they briefly had both. In 1936, having just divorced his wife on account of her adultery with the Earl of

Normanton, he headed for Scarborough and landed specimens of 638 and 595lb. Thus ended his short tunny fishing career, and Prior-Palmer's later life was characterised not by big fish, but by two outspoken decades as Conservative MP for Worthing. He was considered an elder statesman, despite his fervent anti-pacifist stance and, on one occasion, apologising to the House for telling a Labour MP he had 'never done a damned day's work in his life'.

Lady Broughton was a less controversial figure, but no less interesting. Indeed, among the many subjects who sat for painter Philip de Laszlo, few can have been as extraordinary as Vera Edyth Griffith-Boscawen. Lady Broughton, as she later became, was a prominent explorer, big game hunter, fisherwoman and anthropological photographer. Among her many accomplishments, she wrote *Walkabout* with Lord Moyne, based on a six-month trip they took through Burma, Malaysia, Sarawak, Vietnam, the Philippines, China, Papua New Guinea and Australia, covering some 30,000 miles in the process. She also amassed a vast collection of pigmy furniture, later donating it to Pitt-Rivers Museum in Oxford.

Lady Broughton was considered one of the best-dressed women of her generation and when tunny fishing famously slept in a tent on the deck of the drifter *Silver Line*, because she could not bear to go below. Bill Pashby recalls how his father took her fishing before the war, and that 'she used to take ages to land the fish'. Perhaps most surprisingly, however, for anybody who has admired Laszlo's portrait of a beautiful and obviously sophisticated society lady, he adds that 'the language was awful!' Clearly, tunny fishing could test even the most refined characters . . .

Lady Broughton was just one of several talented women to grace Scarborough before the war. In a time when glamorous women and equally elegant yachts were a regular sight, few were more illustrious than *Nahlin*, the yacht owned by Lady Annie Henrietta Yule. It was *Nahlin* in which the Duke of Windsor and Wallis Simpson cruised the Greek Islands before his abdication, although for a time it made its late summer home in the less glamorous waters of the North Sea.

Lady Yule was married to Sir David Yule, a British businessman who spent much of his life, including his married years, in India. Sir David had built Hanstead House, in Hertfordshire, and it was from this base that Lady Yule and daughter Gladys, who herself caught a 623lb tunny in 1933, indulged their interest in animals and big game hunting. Seals, penguins and wallabies were all kept at the house, as was a stuffed bear they had killed in Colorado's Rocky Mountains. In 1925, they started an Arabian horse stud which became famous in its own right, although Lady Yule had many other interests and was a co-founder, with J. Arthur Rank and John Corefield, of Pinewood Studios. Lady Yule died in 1950 but *Nahlin*, the yacht with which she sailed to Scarborough, survives to this day.

Not all of Scarborough's rich visitors, as Horsfall Turner pointed out, had a genuine interest in big game. Baron de Rothschild, for example, preferred to fish for dabs from the deck of his yacht *Eros*, while waiting for his guests to return with their tunny. But Lord Maurice Egerton, fourth Baron Egerton of Tatton, fished off Scarborough for three years, eventually catching a brace of tunny despite chronic seasickness. Uniquely, the entry he made in his Game Book notes that 'These 2 fish were caught on one line. The smaller one got the line caught round its tail, and was landed in 30 minutes, the second one was landed 35 minutes later.' Although not a natural sailor, he had been determined to catch a tunny, and his planning included an extensive list of items to pack for Scarborough. Thus, we now know for posterity that alongside '3 thick vests, 2 thin vests' and '3 flannel shirts', he also took 'Aspirin, lumbago powder, Veg Lax pills, an electric police lantern, a fly swatter and a Libyan desert cummerbund'.

Lord Egerton was a man of considerable wealth, inheriting an estate that had been in his family since the sixteenth century, but his life was ultimately one of the saddest and loneliest of all the tunny anglers. Like many of Scarborough's big game hunters, Lord Egerton was considered a pioneer in several fields. He was an aviator, early motorist, photographer, filmmaker and traveller, but his life was apparently blighted by being spurned, twice, by the only woman he ever loved.

Lord Egerton even built the bizarrely magnificent Egerton Castle in Kenya to impress the unnamed woman, at vast expense. It was a huge, four storey building, with a roof of dressed stones and zinc tiles, every conceivable electrical gadget and an escalator. To celebrate its opening in 1938, Egerton threw one of the biggest parties ever seen in pre-colonial Kenya, but it was all for nought. When the woman for whom the castle had been built finally saw the place, she declared it a museum to his vanity and rejected him for the last time.

It was a turning point in Egerton's life, after which he lived in what has been called a 'fantasy world'. According to an article in the *East African Standard* in 2004, he furnished and ran the castle as if the family he had envisaged actually existed, with nobody but the house servants and occasional guests allowed to enter. Egerton also developed a passionate hatred of women, with warning signs around the castle stating that female trespassers would be shot, and guests with wives and daughters were asked to leave them eight miles from the castle. When he planned to visit the quarters where his African staff lived, Egerton gave them two weeks' notice so that all women could be moved elsewhere. Even by the standards of the notorious 'Happy Valley' set, this was eccentric in the extreme.

Egerton died childless in 1958. He was the last in the family line, but his legacy includes the Egerton University in Njoro, which he founded, and the Cheshire family seat of Tatton Park, which he bequeathed to the National Trust. It is here, with his collection of big game, that Lord Egerton's two tunny can still be seen. Perhaps the final word on Egerton, however, should be left to F. B. Hannam, or rather the crewman that Hannam overheard while he and Egerton were vainly hunting tunny in 1931. Egerton had succumbed to seasickness and made his customary deposit in the North Sea, only to manfully strap on the harness and prepare to do battle - despite his obvious nausea. On seeing this one of the crew turned to his colleague and said, in a remark that briefly confused Hannam, 'The Lord is a wonderful man'.

Seasickness aside, Egerton did at least catch a brace, even if one of them wasn't properly hooked. Many other visitors to Scarborough blanked or, in the case of The Lord Lovat, landed only one tunny. Lord Lovat's fish was a middleweight of 560lb, caught in 1934, but he was no less interesting a character for that. Born as Simon Fraser in 1911, but known to his associates as Shimi, he was educated at Ampleforth College and attended Oxford University. After graduation in 1932 he was commissioned into the Scots Guards. His father, who had founded the Lovat Scouts during the Boer War, died in 1933, and so Simon Fraser succeeded him to become the seventeenth Baron Lovat, chief of the Fraser Clan.

When the Second World War began, Lovat volunteered for one of the newly formed Commando units - perhaps unsurprisingly, since his cousin was no less a man than David Stirling, who later founded the Special Air Service. Both men were apparently singled out by Hitler as 'dangerous terrorists' and orders had been issued for them to be executed if captured.

Lovat's first action came in March 1941, with the Lofoten Raid. It was an enormous success, but in August 1942, now as a Lieutenant-Colonel, Lovat took part in the ill-fated Dieppe Raid. The raid was a complete disaster, for a number of reasons, but Lovat's planning was particularly praised, later leading one Canadian officer to remark that, for his rank and role, he possessed perhaps the finest military brain of the war.

When the Normandy invasion drew near, Lord Lovat was promoted to Brigadier and given charge of the 1st Special Service Brigade. On 12th June, however, a stray shell from 51st

Highland Division fell short, killing Lieutenant-Colonel Johnson of the 12th Battalion and severely injuring Lord Lovat. Lieutenant-Colonel Derek Mills-Roberts later said of the injured man that 'He was in a frightful mess; a large shell fragment had cut deeply into his back and side . . . He was very calm. "Take over the brigade," he said, "and whatever happens - not a foot back." He repeated this several times. And then, "Get me a priest," he said.

Lord Lovat entered the political arena in 1945 as Under-Secretary of State for Foreign Affairs. In early 1945, with the defeat of Germany now inevitable, he was sent to meet Stalin as part of a diplomatic offensive. Churchill wrote to Stalin and informed him that Lord Lovat was 'the mildest-mannered man that ever scuttled a ship or cut a throat'. He might have added, had he even known, that Lovat was also one of the most accomplished men ever to battle a tunny.

Another military heavyweight to try for a tunny was Wing Commander Edward Hedley Fielden, who found time to boat a brace in 1938 despite a busy flying career. In 1926, he had been plucked from RAF No. 23 Squadron to be Personal Pilot to HRH The Prince of Wales, later King Edward VIII, a role which involved flying the Prince's private Gypsy Moth G-AAKV. 'Mouse' Fielden, as he was known, later became Captain of the King's Flight on Edward's ascension in 1936, in addition to Equerry in Waiting.

Even the abdication crisis, holidays in Scarborough and the outbreak of war had little effect on Mouse's seemingly gilded career. He continued as Captain of the King's Flight under George VI, remaining as its commander when it was absorbed into No. 161 Squadron. 161's wartime role was to deliver and pick up agents operating behind enemy lines, and in 1943, Fielden was awarded the Distinguished Flying Cross. His Citation, published in the *London Gazette*, said Fielden had 'flown on various operational missions, some of a most hazardous nature . . . setting an example which has contributed materially

Some notable tunny fishers . . .

Sir Miles Lampson.

Lord Lovat.
Photo taken in 1942.

Sir Edward 'Mouse'
Fielden.

T.O.M. Sopwith
(*Library of Congress*)

to the high morale of the air crews under his command'.

In a club of such conspicuously brilliant achievers, though, even Fielden's flying career was eclipsed. But then T.O.M. Sopwith, pioneering aviator, racing car driver, motorboat champion and one of the fathers of the jet age, would have stood out in the most illustrious of company.

Sopwith's interest in flying began in 1906, when he was eighteen. He was racing cars at Brooklands airfield and became fascinated by the planes he saw there, buying a Howard Wright monoplane of his own soon after. On his first flight, he crashed. Undaunted, he then bought a biplane and soon obtained his pilot's certificate, number 31. Before long, however, Sopwith was building his own biplanes, and the War Office ordered a dozen.

It was during the First World War that Sopwith really made his name, helping secure Britain's air supremacy with the Snipe, Salamander, Pup, Dolphin and legendary Camel. After the war, more success followed, developing military aircraft with Harry Hawker. Sopwith later bought Gloster Aircraft and established the Hawker Siddeley Group, producing the famous Hurricane, which played a pivotal role in the Battle of Britain, and the only operational Allied jet fighter of World War II, the Meteor.

Sopwith, who was knighted in 1953, can be reasonably said to have influenced both World Wars with his planes. Between the two, however, while building his aviation business, he also found time to chase tunny in Scarborough. In the first week of September 1933, during a record week for the British Tunny Club, he landed five, including fish of 720 and 740lb, while Mrs Sopwith acquitted herself well with three tunny to 650lb. It was an impressive performance by anybody's standards, but for a man as used to winning as Tommy Sopwith, it was hardly a surprise.

Other famous industrialists tried their hand at tunny fishing, albeit with less success. One such was Kenneth MacAlpine, a scion of the civil engineering dynasty first started by Robert

MacAlpine in 1869. 'Concrete Bob', as he was known, made his fortune developing cost-effective construction techniques which found their way into roads, railways and, most notably, the first Wembley Stadium. This family wealth enabled Kenneth to indulge his passion for motor racing, and by 1951, he had established the Connaught marque. Connaught excelled with Formula 2 cars but was rarely able to compete with the continental works teams at Grand Prix level. MacAlpine did race himself, but by 1955, his business commitments had forced him to give up professional driving without ever succeeding at the highest level. Alas, the same was true of his big game career. Despite being a prominent member of the British Tunny Club in its final years, he never made his mark in the North Sea or gained one of their coveted certificates.

Of all the rich sports to visit Scarborough, however, few did more for the local fishermen than H. E. Weatherley, of Teddington, who first caught a tunny in 1934 but was by far the most prolific angler of the post-war tunny years. He formed a particular bond with the Pashby family, catching the majority of his fish from the keel boat *Courage*. Bill Pashby, who as a young boy went on many of Weatherley's jaunts, recalls that like Lady Broughton, Weatherley was reluctant to venture below decks, and like many of the tunny fraternity, he had his eccentricities. 'Mr Weatherley had a proper tent on deck,' he recalls. 'He wouldn't go below. Ninety per cent of his food was fruit. You know, them baby tins. And he always had a fag going.'

His fastidious nature was not confined to his time afloat. On one occasion, young Bill accompanied him to the bank in Scarborough, where Weatherley wanted to draw out £500. The female assistant brought him the money, but the used banknotes were not to his taste. "Take that dirty money away," he demanded, "I want new!"

H. E. Weatherley was, however, a generous client. Bill's father William had admired a boat, the *Nan McMurray*, and

Weatherley with a brace of big fish in 1953.

Weatherley offered to buy it for him. Pashby Senior declined, later telling his son that 'he didn't want to be beholden'. Weatherley also offered to double whatever Pashby was earning from his usual fishing, in order to secure the services of his favourite tunny skipper. Clearly, he was a determined man, prepared to spend considerable sums of money to catch his quarry, although even he didn't manage to catch everything he wanted. 'Bear in mind there was whales there too,' adds Bill Pashby. 'Mr Weatherley always wanted to catch one.'

It was Mr Weatherley who gave a trophy to William Pashby in 1949, in recognition of his huge contribution to the tunny years, and the same Mr Weatherley who hosted a party for Scarborough's tunny skippers. He may have been a wealthy southerner, but few outsiders got as close to - or were as accepted by - Scarborough's fishermen. Writing in *The Art of Angling*, Eric Horsfall Turner said of him: 'The average weight of his fish is about 625lb. No doubt Mr Weatherley would be the first to grant some of the credit for this remarkable achievement to his skipper, Will Pashby of keel boat *Courage* . . . but although the skipper is of invaluable assistance in finding fish, he neither plays them when hooked nor supplies the unswerving persistence necessary to such an achievement. Mr Weatherley has shown . . . good weather or not, a determined angler can bring back fish from the North Sea with almost monotonous regularity.'

10

A Broken Record

Wasn't it rather foolish of him to start by fishing for tunny?

Of all the *arrivistes* who turned up in Scarborough each summer, none were quite so successful, or as unwittingly contentious, as John Hedley Lewis. He only fished once in his life, in 1949, but the result was a controversy which has never been satisfactorily resolved.

John Hedley Lewis was not a man to do things by halves. He competed twice in the doubles at Wimbledon, gained a First in mathematics from Cambridge, piloted planes before the war and was a renowned skier. When hostilities broke out, he served in RAF intelligence and was on duty when the call came through for the Dambusters raid. Small wonder, then, that when he turned his hand to fishing, the results were spectacular.

His son, Vincent, remembers it well. 'It was just before I went off to school,' he recalls from his Lincolnshire estate. 'Father was coming up from a meeting in London and was sat next to this chap on the train. They got talking about tunny fishing and this chap suggested he come up to Scarborough and give it a go.'

As his father packed what he would need for the trip, the young Vincent asked him where he was going. "I'm going to

catch the biggest fish ever caught," was the reply.

'He got back on the train,' adds Vincent, 'met up with his friend and went to hire a rod and reel. I remember he bought a crate of beer to swap for a crate of herring. Soon after 7pm he went out, and then they got into the rowing boat. After about twenty minutes he hooked the fish.'

The tunny went off 'like a train', its first run proving too much for the brake on the hired reel. Eventually the fish sounded, as many big tunny did, expiring dozens of fathoms down on the sea bed. Hedley Lewis' boatman suggested he cut the line, but the novice was determined not to lose the first fish he had ever hooked. Applying some of his mathematical thinking to the task, he worked out a technique for rapidly lowering the rod, winding hard as he did so, gradually hauling the tunny towards the surface. An hour and a half later, it was gaffed and on its way to Scarborough.

'I think they got back at about half past two in the morning,' says Vincent. 'There was nobody around to weigh it so it just hung there until around six in the morning, losing blood, until it could be weighed.' Later that morning, Vincent's mother told him some exciting news - his father was on the radio. The story was all about a Lincolnshire farmer who had caught a new record tunny of 852lb . . .

Indeed he had. When the tunny was eventually put on the scales it beat Lorenzo Mitchell-Henry's fish by just one pound, thus becoming the largest fish ever caught off the Scarborough coast - for a while at least.

John Hedley Lewis, a hastily-recruited member of the British Tunny Club, was awarded four trophies, for biggest fish of the 1949 season, biggest fish caught from a boat under forty-five feet, biggest fish caught on Hardy's tackle and biggest fish by a novice. The capture also appeared in the 1950 *Guinness Book of Records*, but a small storm was brewing in the wood-panelled rooms of certain London clubs. In March 1950, the *Fishing Gazette*, quoting the British Tunny Club's 1949 report, said

Hedley Lewis and his disputed record fish.

'the largest fish of the season turned the scale at 852lb'. From the Carlton Club, in St James's Street, a Mr H. Underdown wrote to question the weighing of the fish, stating that 'If it was from a hook and knotted piece of heavy hawser the weight recorded would not be the weight of the fish. The present record, I understand 851lb, was recorded on the slab of a railway weighing machine, obviously the only really accurate method.'

Meanwhile, over at the RAC Club, the previous record holder was doing his best to have the weight of the Hedley Lewis fish discredited. Not for the first time, nor even the second, Lorenzo Mitchell-Henry was casting doubt on the validity of a new record fish. 'I have seen many tunny weighed at Scarborough,' he wrote in the *Fishing Gazette*, 'but never considered their recorded weights as being more than an approximation.'

'Of the 200 tunny recorded in club annuals between the years 1930 and 1948, there are only two of correct weight,' he added, '*viz.* those caught by me.'

The issue, argued Mitchell-Henry, was that while he had weighed his 1930 and 1931 fish on railway slab scales, the British Tunny Club, from whom he had long since failed to hide his hostility, weighed their fish by suspending them off the ground on a short length of rope. 'I trust the Tunny Club,' finished Mitchell-Henry, 'will now abandon its untenable position.'

Others soon joined the fray, via the letters page of the *Fishing Gazette*. F. W. Olphert speculated that the fish may have weighed rather more, but then again may not have, while the Reverend D. A. Ryce Roberts, of Scarborough took a rather more decisive view: 'The 1949 tunny was weighed on scales suspended by a rope, or "becket". By some oversight the rope was not weighed independently at the time. It has been calculated that the smallest length of rope required to suspend a fish of over 850lb would weigh 1¾lb when dry, and about 2½lb when wet. Since there was only 1lb difference in weight between these two splendid fish, the weight of the rope must enter into any claim as to which was the heavier fish.'

'The present position must be unsatisfactory,' he concluded, 'both to Mr J. H. Lewis . . . and to Mr Mitchell-Henry. A statement from the Tunny Club would clarify the position.'

No such statement was forthcoming, at least publicly, but Mitchell-Henry sensed victory. Vincent Hedley Lewis recalls that his father received letters from Mitchell-Henry's lawyers at around this time, while early in 1951, the *Fishing Gazette* published perhaps the most unsavoury missive of the whole affair. 'As Mr Taylor was present at the weighing of Mr Lewis's fish,' asked Mitchell-Henry, 'is he prepared to sign an affidavit before a notary public to the effect that the 852lb claimed was all fish and nothing extraneous had been added to its net weight? It is noted with satisfaction that he is determined strictly to enforce the rules of his club. This being so, will he pledge his word that the captor of the fish had been elected a member of the club, in conformity with Rule 5, *viz*: (I) that he had applied for membership in a letter to the committee. (II) that letters from his sponsors had been received by the honorary secretaries. (III) that he was proposed and seconded by two full members of the club. (IV) that he was elected a member of the club before he caught his fish?'

Quite why Hedley Lewis' membership of the British Tunny Club so concerned Mitchell-Henry is unknown. He was not himself a member, either in 1951 or when he had caught his 851lb fish, and had long called for the disbandment of the club. Whatever his motivation, Mitchell-Henry seemed determined to pursue the matter, through the courts if necessary, but neither Fred Taylor nor John Hedley Lewis rose to his bait. The latter, in particular, had maintained a dignified silence, happy simply to have caught a very big fish. 'Father,' said Vincent Hedley Lewis, referring to the fuss, 'couldn't be bothered with it all.'

The *Fishing Gazette*, however, having allowed its letters page to fuel the debate, felt it had to make a decision one way or

John Hedley Lewis with the British Tunny Club Cups, 1949. The cups were for the following:
1. Biggest Fish for the 1949 season.
2. Biggest Fish from a boat under 45 feet.
3. Biggest Fish using Hardy's Tackle.
4. Biggest Fish by a novice.

another. On 1st September, 1951, it printed a short statement which seemingly brought an end to the discussion: 'This fish, stated to weigh 852lb, is described as a British record. In the *Fishing Gazette*, 2nd September, 1950, we pointed out that this fish was suspended on the scales by a rope or "becket" and the weight of this included in the 852lb. In view of this it cannot be accepted as beating the existing record of 851lb held by Mr L. Mitchell-Henry since 1933.'

So what of the fish which caused all this trouble? John Hedley Lewis had it set up and for years, it sat in the hall of his Lincolnshire home, a rather large reminder of his brief angling career. When Vincent inherited, the tunny came too, although he eventually tired of it and put it into storage. Some years later, his wife found it languishing in a garage on the estate and they contacted the Scarborough Museums Trust, who offered to put it on public display.

The fish soon became the centrepiece of the Wood End Museum's extensive tunny archive, which also included original photographs, log books, cups, certificates, medals and other ephemera. By now the tunny was looking rather careworn, so frozen chip manufacturer McCain Foods offered £2,500 to have it restored to its former glory. It was restored and a fibreglass cast made, but with the closure of the Wood End Museum, the tunny and its twin were confined to the Trust's storage facility, away from prying eyes.

As to the true weight of the Hedley Lewis fish, we will never really know. It certainly looks huge, even now, but whether it is the biggest or second biggest tunny landed at Scarborough is impossible to say. Its captor never fished again, nor did anybody from the Tunny Club emerge to settle the matter once and for all. According to Bill Pashby, though, whose father helped land the monster, 'there was nothing wrong with the weight of that fish'.

If Lorenzo Mitchell-Henry were still with us, of course, he might disagree . . .

11

The Last Hurrah
1945 - 1954

Every fin, except the slotted dorsal, was hard at work.
I never want to see anything finer.

Unsurprisingly, the Second World War brought tunny fishing to a close. For six long years, the idea of taking to a perilous North Sea in the name of sport was not just unwise, but utterly irreverent. And besides, both the men and vessels at the heart of the sport were needed elsewhere. Many, of course, did not return.

Although hostilities effectively ceased in August 1945, just in time for the tunny's arrival, no fish were landed in East Coast ports that year. Men and boats were in short supply and it would take more than a few weeks to get the sport's complex logistics in place once more. The British Tunny Club, however, had continued to tick over, and in March 1946 the Club published a brief report for the war years. It had retained a healthy bank balance and the use of its Sandgate facilities, but was less optimistic about the availability of charter boats for its members. The situation would probably improve, it said, by the time the tunny arrived in August. It even speculated that it may have to change its name, after two broadbill swordfish were seen off Scarborough.

An exchange of letters in the *Fishing Gazette* also hinted at broadening horizons. Sven Somme wrote to report that huge stocks of 'Cornish' tunny were being seen off Norway and, armed with Fred Taylor's 'beginner's' guide, he had tried his hand. Somme's efforts were in vain, however, and he finished by adding that 'My rod is now for sale'. Fred Taylor responded, tongue firmly in cheek and aghast that his book should be considered as a useful guide to success - particularly as no mention of Cornish tunny was made in its pages. He did, however, admit to trying for a tunny off Cornwall himself, without success.

As the world recovered from war, the mood among tunny anglers was cautiously optimistic. There was no reason, they felt, why the East Coast's - or Cornwall's - best years were not still ahead of them, if only suitable boats could be found. Little did they know the sport was entering its glorious, but ultimately brief, final chapter.

On 25th August, 1946, Mr Norman D. Lees, of Middlesbrough, who was also curiously the British Tunny Club's Honorary Argentine Correspondent, landed the first post-war tunny, a comparative middleweight of 530lb. Fishing from the *Georgiana*, a converted Brixham trawler owned by Michael Wild, Lees hooked his fish some fifty miles E.N.E. of Scarborough and landed it after a forty-five minute tussle, earning himself a Grey Seal Certificate from the British Tunny Club. On the same day, his host and another guest, a Dr Dieter, had also hooked a tunny apiece, but failed to land them. Clearly, the fish were still there in numbers.

The following day, 26th August, Tunny Club stalwart Captain C. H. Frisby VC and Colonel L. Sadler chartered Tom Pashby's *Our Maggie* and headed out to sea. Frisby fished from a small rowing boat while Sadler, ignoring the advice of Mitchell-Henry and others, tried his luck from the tender. Remarkably, both men hooked tunny at the same time, giving themselves an interesting problem. It was normal practice for

Sir E. T. Peel and his September 1949 fish.

the parent vessel to follow the rowing boat, but the chances of both fish heading in the same direction were slim. Colonel Sadler was anxious not to lose sight of his colleague, who was battling a decent fish from a much smaller boat, and quickly hand-lined his 474lb tunny to the gaff. It was the first time a tunny had been landed from such a large boat, a notable if not entirely sporting achievement, and in doing so Sadler forfeited his Tunny Club certificate.

Frisby's fish weighed two pounds more than his colleague's, and together the brace were exhibited at Scarborough. In all, some 3,256 people paid to see them, raising £40 for local charities. Scarborough's fascination with tunny, it seemed, was as strong as ever.

Large numbers of tunny were still being seen off Scarborough during September, although some of the pre-war fishing boats were now providing more lucrative pleasure trips, and anglers found charters hard to come by. The lucky few who had their own boats, however, had feeding tunny to themselves. One such was Michael Wild, who, having lost a tunny in August, returned with his *Georgiana* to make amends. He did not take long. On 2nd September, his boat docked at Whitby flying two Tunny Club pennants.

Wild had found feeding tunny just nine miles off Whitby, hooking his fish at 5.25am. 'It gave me a great fight,' he told the *Fishing Gazette* later that day, 'leading me a _____ of a dance. I played it in the early stages with great caution, for I was desperately anxious to land a tunny. There were many anxious moments as the fish tried to break away, and four times it dragged my small craft round in a complete circle. There were no Dutch fishing vessels in the vicinity, so no danger of my fish getting away under the keel of any craft. It was a straightforward fight, and I cannot describe my excitement as I realised I had made sure of landing the fish. The strain was tremendous, but it was well worthwhile, and I hope to be fishing again tonight.'

Wild's tunny was the first landed at Whitby since the war and

Jack Tansey and crew.

On August 20th, 1949, Fred Taylor caught this splendid tunny of 694lb.
Conditions were just perfect and he landed his fish after a forty-five minute fight.

weighed 592lb on the scales at Whitby Railway Station. The fish's weight was certified by Captain J. L. Hardy, of the British Tunny Club, before it was returned to the quayside, along with a smaller fish taken by Wild's companion, Miss Maureen Lees. The fish were then exhibited to the public, in return for donations to the Whitby branch of the Royal National Lifeboat Institute.

Nor did Wild's success end there. On 7th September, he caught two more fish, weighing 586 and 567lb, bringing his total of Grey Seal Certificates for the month to three. On the same day, Captain Frisby also caught a brace of 500-pounders, before returning on 26th September to take the last, and smallest certified fish of the season, weighing 476lb. Given a dire shortage of boats, poor availability of tackle and incessant bad weather, it was as successful a season as anybody had reasonably hoped for.

The 1947 season opened in fine style. A warm summer meant herring were abundant in the North Sea by early August, with large catches made by the drifters. Naturally, the tunny followed in their wake, and local hotelier Tom Laughton took full advantage. In a remarkable morning's sport, he hooked four and landed three, weighing 785, 707 and 536lb - a year to the day since Frisby and Sadler had enjoyed their simultaneous battles.

Sadly, the 1947 season did not fulfil its early promise. Boats remained scarce and only five other tunny were recorded, all of them single captures. J.H. Hamer landed a 602lb fish, with J. A. Tansey and H. E. Weatherley managing 526 and 543lb respectively. The real highlight, however, was Dr Bidi Evans, whose 714lb specimen, caught fishing from her father's yacht, remains the British women's record to this day.

The 1948 season almost never arrived. The British Tunny Club was bullish and had raised its subscription fees from £1 1s to £3 3s, to cover expenditure on 'renewals and replenishments', but by the end of August, not one tunny had been landed. On 3rd September, however, Fred Taylor arrived in

Scarborough, determined to make amends. 'Well the old firm of Tom Birch and myself is still, apparently, ticking over,' he wrote, three days later, 'and I was lucky to get hooked into a fish at 5.30 a.m. this morning. Weight 644lb. We had a battle royal and it was pure, unadulterated hell for the fifty minutes it took to get him to the boat. I feel remarkably stiff and sore this morning!'

'Never, so far as I remember, since tunny fishing started,' he continued, 'has the season been so late. Fish have always been caught before this. This has, I think, been entirely due to the weather, which has been so bad this year and has affected many other things than tunny fishing.'

Taylor's fish was widely publicised as the first tunny of the 1948 season, but J. A. Tansey had also landed a fish of 508lb on the 6th, and it was not until October that he tried to clear up the confusion. His fish, he explained, was gaffed and brought aboard by 4am, an hour and a half before Taylor's epic battle had started. Tansey would not have troubled to point this out, he explained, but one of his crew had placed a substantial wager on the first tunny of the season, and the loser required a letter in the *Fishing Gazette* before paying up . . .

Tansey's morning was further enlivened by the antics of his skipper, Ernie Williamson, eschewing such niceties as a rod and reel to catch a tunny 'Spanish fashion'. The capture would hardly gain Williamson a certificate from No. 1 Sandgate, but it did provide Tansey with a chance to watch a fighting tunny at very close quarters. 'We saw everything it had while it was very much alive,' he wrote, 'its beautiful colour showing to perfection in the new daylight - iridescent silver of the armour plated looking head and sides, plus tinges of mauve and duck egg blue merging into the very dark back.'

The season's tally was now two legitimately-caught tunny. Bad weather then kept anglers on dry land for two days, but late on the 8th, both Tansey and Taylor headed back out in their respective boats. Taylor was clearly still recovering from his earlier success, a fish which had tested him to the limit. 'I can think of no fish which gave me such a fight,' he later recalled. 'He darn well nearly killed me!' Even so, Taylor was keen to repeat the exercise, and soon found himself in among the herring fleet's deck lights - 'It looked just like Piccadilly Circus.'

Two fish were quickly hooked and lost, the second and larger of the two due to a line frayed by previous encounters. He and Tom Birch were furious but fished on, soon hooking a third fish which fought well but not, mercifully, as hard as the first fish of the week. By a strange coincidence, it also weighed 644lb when it was eventually brought ashore, but the battle was notable more for the comedy of errors at its climax. Taylor, ever happy to have fun at his own expense, was good enough to share the details in the *Fishing Gazette*: 'We had a frightful job getting him aboard. You never saw such a mess up. We got him about half way up all right. There were four of us on the rope - then I slipped and Bob Allen, my boatman, fell on the top of me and the third member of the crew fell on him! You never saw anything like it! Thank goodness my precious glasses weren't smashed in the process. I think it took us over half an hour of valuable time to get that wretched fish aboard.'

Tansey's morning was even more eventful, with three tunny to 623lb, the biggest of which took almost two and a half hours to bring to the gaff. He told the *Fishing Gazette* that 'anybody would have caught fish this week', but 1948 had ended with just six fish landed, by two anglers on only two days. Several fish had been lost, nine of them by Tansey, but it was still a far cry from the huge pre-war catches. Prospects for 1949 did not look good.

Once again, however, the tunny were about to surprise everybody.

Having failed, just, to land the first tunny of the 1948 season, Fred Taylor was an early visitor to Scarborough in 1949. For once, conditions were just right, and on 20th August, he succeeded in landing a tunny of 694lb after a forty-five-minute

Horsfall Turner with skipper Ernie Williamson and the crew of the Shirley Williamson, *1949. Inset: President of the British Tunny Club, Saville Cohen and a 1949 fish.*

Tom Laughton posing with the crew of the Our Maggie.

fight. The capture featured in Hardy adverts in the angling press, with a brief message congratulating Taylor on 'again' (*sic*) catching the first tunny of the season, under the heading 'Hardy Tackle will certainly hold 'em'.

They had ample opportunity to live up to this boast in 1949. For the first time since the war, tunny were not just plentiful, but accessible to more than a handful of anglers. The result was not one, but two pages in the British Tunny Club's list of certified fish. Fred Taylor himself finished with three fish, the best going 740lb, but it was H. E. Weatherley who led the way with an astonishing eleven tunny. His best weighed 701lb, but it was his multiple captures of four fish on 25th August, and three more on the 27th, that most captured the imagination.

Among the anglers in Scarborough that year was well known Australian fisherman Dr A. B. K. Watkins, of New South Wales, who landed two tunny, including a 696lb specimen on 130lb line, a Tunny Club record in the Blue Seal category. Several other anglers, some of them new names to the sport,

were successful that year. R. Bradlaw landed five, J. A. Tansey
boated nine and Sir E. T. Peel and Eric Horsfall Turner both
managed a leash apiece. Saville Cohen landed two, the biggest
of which was a leviathan of 749lb, while C. N. Weatherby,
H. N. Charrington, L. Kirkby, J. M. Peel, D. F. Peel and J.
Hedley Lewis all had one each. It was this last fish, originally
weighed in at a British record-beating 852lb, which was to
prove more contentious than any other tunny caught in the
North Sea.

But that particular argument would have to wait. For the time
being, spirits were high and the British Tunny Club's end of
year report for 1949 struck a suitably buoyant tone: 'In great
contrast to 1948, 1949 came up to expectations. Many early
enquiries were made for boats by old and new members and
tunny were reported in late July and early August within 20
miles. Anglers appeared reluctant to make a start until after
receiving an SOS Fred Taylor came post haste from Surrey and
again caught the first fish of the season . . . from then on to
September 23 a succession of anglers, mostly new members,
but quite a few of the old members, including the Club's first
President, Sir Edward T. Peel, KBE, DSO, MC, had a grand
time.'

'During the season tunny were never more than 6 to 8 miles
from the coast and they appeared to be present in greater numbers than ever before. Forty-six fish were landed at an average
weight of 606lb. The Tunny Charity Fund raised £700 by the
exhibition of tunny caught by members and after clearing
expenses and buying a new exhibition hut, £500 was dis-
tributed to seventeen local charities.'

On 22nd August, 1950, H. E. Weatherley got the new season
under way. Fishing from Bill Pashby's *Courage*, 35 miles north-
east of Scarborough, he hooked a tunny in the early hours,
subduing it in an hour and twelve minutes. Just before 5am,
he hooked a second, bringing it to the gaff in less than an hour.
The brace later weighed 560 and 561lb when weighed at the

West Pier, although their combined weight proved too much for the motor on the crane which tried, unwisely perhaps, to lift both fish on to the dock at the same time.

Never one to be satisfied with just a couple of tunny, Weatherley returned to the fray two days later. He managed four fish this time, two middleweights and a pair over the 700lb mark. In reporting the catch, the *Fishing Gazette* reminded would-be tunny anglers to weigh their catches carefully, particularly if they should be lucky to break the 850lb mark. A storm was now brewing over the Hedley Lewis fish of the previous year.

But any fears of another controversy were unfounded. Sir Edward Peel was the only other angler to successfully boat a tunny that year, a fish of 639lb landed on 2nd September which brought the 1950 season to an early finish.

If 1950 had been disappointing, 1951 was even more so. Only four tunny were landed, a leash for the ever-persistent Harry Weatherley, and a fish of 642lb for E. T. Wasdell. Wasdell's tunny was a controversial capture, however, and led to a furious letter from H. E. Weatherley to Fred Taylor and Frank Watkinson. 'Because it was not caught from a row-boat,' wrote Weatherley, 'it does not qualify for a certificate . . . for goodness' sake let us apply the rules as they have been followed since the club was formed. The next thing we will hear is that someone has caught a fish from a helicopter, and, because this is specifically not mentioned in the rules, it will qualify. Don't let us give people like M.H. another opportunity to raise a storm, on the strength of saying we stretch the rules to suit a particular case.'

The following year saw seven tunny landed, including fish of 742 and 747lb, but all seven fish came to Weatherley's rod. Those few others who made the effort caught nothing.

The British Tunny Club, keen to recruit new anglers to the sport, embarked on a publicity drive. It even persuaded the BBC to overcome its institutional indifference to angling, and was granted four and a half minutes of airtime on its 'Eye Witness' radio programme. Club President Colonel

It's a poor fish

—that doesn't know

SCARBOROUG
THE FISHERMAN'S PARAD

For here is fishing in abundance. Salt or fresh water. From the
trout to the powerful, fighting tunny. Here, in the waters of S
—is the angler's dream.

The British Tunny Fishing Club operates from its Headquarters at Scarbc
miles of fine Trout and Grayling fishing, controlled by the Derwent A
(Founded 1839), in the nearby Yorkshire Derwent. Excellent coarse fishing in !
Mere. From the Marine Drive, the East Pier—or from cobles—codling, flat f
whiting, and mackerel. And . . . that great national angling event—S
Annual Angling Festival in September.

A copy of our new folder "Angling at Scarborough" will gladly be ser

For further details write to:—

THE PUBLICITY DEPT, TOWN HALL, SCARBOR

*You can't
exaggerate
the
possibilities of*

Scarborough

For sea or fresh-water fishing Scarborough is the
sportsman's paradise. National centre for Tunny
fishing, the British Tunny Fishing Club controls
the sport from its Scarborough headquarters.

The Derwent Anglers Club (Founded 1839) controls
ten miles of excellent Trout and Grayling fishing in
the Yorkshire Derwent near Scarborough, set in lovely
and peaceful surroundings. The lower reaches of the
Derwent, the Costa and Pickering Beck also afford
good sport. At the Scarborough Mere the coarse
fishing is excellent.

Fishing from the Marine Drive, East Pier and from
cobles provides good sport including codling, flat fish,
gurnard, whiting and mackerel (according to season).

The annual Angling Festival in September attracts
keen anglers from all parts of Britain.

For further details required write to—
THE INFORMATION CENTRE
St. Nicholas Street, Scarborough, Yorks.

★ *852 lbs. in weight, nearly 9 feet long
and 6 feet in girth, the record Tunny
was landed at Scarborough in 1949.*

The first thing you feel is a violent tug on your line,
a tug that quickly builds up and you say to yourself: "I've
hooked one". And then the line shrills out for two or three
hundred yards; the bows of your boat begin to swing round in the
direction the fish is taking, and the fight is "on". When your
line has run out for two or three hundred yards you begin to put
a brake on it, and then the line goes slack and you settle down
and lean back in your harness, with the fish towing your dinghy
at four or five miles an hour.

It's really a case of man against fish, a fish weighing six
or seven hundred pounds and perhaps a good deal more, and your only
weapon is a six-foot rod - possibly with a steel centre, but still
only a rod. You're sitting up in the bows of the dinghy with the
heel of the rod resting in a cup on the seat between your legs,
and you wear a harness. But you're not harnessed to the boat, only
to your rod, so that you can bring the whole strength of your shoulders
and back to bear in the struggle, but your harness is fitted with a
quick release gear in case of emergency.

*George Baker's
radio script.*

for eye witness

Speaker: Col. George Baker (not staff)
Title: Tunny Fishing
Duration: 4'25"
Origin & date: 1A - Egton House, 23rd August 1951
Passed by:
TA/PT

CUE: The tunny fishing season in the North Sea has once again opened,
with the first fish landed at Scarborough. We've asked a tunny
fisherman - George Baker - he's President of the British Tunny Club -
to tell Eye Witness listeners what it's like playing a fish that may
weigh anything up to one thousand pounds. Incidentally, he has only
just returned from captaining the British team which fished against
Sweden and Denmark this week. (N.B. Colonel Baker specifically asks
to be introduced as plain "George Baker", this being tunny fishing
etiquette).

BAKER: The first thing you feel is a violent tug on your line, a tug
that quickly builds up and you say to yourself: "I've hooked one".
And then the line shrills out for two or three hundred yards; the bows
of your boat begin to swing round in the direction the fish is taking,
and the fight is "on". When your line starts running out you begin to
put a brake on it, and then it goes taut and you settle down and lean
back in your harness, with a fish of anything up to nine hundred pounds
towing your dinghy at four or five miles an hour.

Your only weapon is a six-foot rod - possibly with a steel centre,
but still only a rod. You're sitting up in the bows of the dinghy with
the heel of the rod in a cup on the seat between your legs, and you wear
a harness. But you're not harnessed to the boat, only to your rod, so
that you can bring the whole strength of your shoulders and back to bear
in the struggle, but your harness is fitted with a quick release gear in
case of emergency. We set out information where the tunny are from the
men of the trawler and drifter fleets. By that time we're already at
sea in a Scarborough fishing boat - usually a thirty-five footer with a
small engine - with your dinghy in tow, heading towards the drifter
fleet. Once there you clamber into the dinghy, set up your rod, bait your hook
with a mackerel or herring and await events.

Once you've booked a fish you can never really say what'll happen.
It took me only fifty-five minutes to bring in one tunny. On the
other hand, I've played a fish for nine hours. The biggest fish I
caught towed me away out of sight of the fleet. I was so intent on
the game that I didn't realise what was happening until it struck me
that my boatman had suddenly gone a bit quiet. When I called over my
shoulder, "what's the matter," he said: "Nothing, Sir, but don't look
round just now." Well, of course I did look round, when I found we
were way out to sea without so much as a sail in sight. But all ended
well, because our fishing boat came alongside just as I caught my
fish - the biggest tunny I've ever caught: it weighed seven hundred
and sixty-three pounds.

You can never be sure what a tunny is going to do. When it realises
it's hooked it surges forward and you can feel the strain on your arms
and back. The creature slackens off again and again, and each time
you wonder if your thin line will hold. It's only about as thick as a
matchstick. On one occasion a whale surfaced, close to the dinghy - in
fact so close that I actually patted it on the back. But I've never
known a hooked tunny come as close as this. When it begins to tire it may
start circling the boat, and then suddenly it zigzags off for the last
time and you know you've won. It may be necessary to bring it up from
the sea bottom and believe me this can be tiring work. You strain upwards on your rod, drop the point and reel-in. Perhaps this straining
up and reeling-in can go on for a couple of hours, but you have an
adequate reward in the first sight of your tunny. It lies in the water
an incredibly beautiful sight, anything up to nine feet of shimmering
gold and green and purple and silver, a beautiful thing, shaped like a
torpedo - fat in the middle and slender at the tail, with a blunt nose
like that of a mackerel. When you haul it aboard the fishing boat that
took you out the irridescence slowly fades. You can watch it fading,

[174]

Baker - who, according to the original script, asked to be referred to as plain George Baker, 'this being tunny fishing etiquette' - gave listeners a passionate essay on chasing tunny:

The first thing you feel is a violent tug on your line, a tug that quickly builds up and you say to yourself, 'I've hooked one.' And then the line shrills out for two or three hundred yards; the bows of your boat begin to swing round in the direction the fish is taking, and the fight is on. When your line starts running out you begin to put a brake on it, and then it goes taut and you settle down and lean back in your harness, with a fish of anything up to nine hundred pounds towing your dinghy at four or five miles an hour.

Your only weapon is a six foot rod - possibly with a steel centre, but still only a rod. You're sitting up in the bows of the dinghy the heel of the rod in a cup on the seat between your legs, and you wear a harness. But you're not harnessed to the boat, only to your rod, so that you can bring the whole strength of your shoulders and back to bear in the struggle, but your harness is fitted with a quick release gear in case of emergency.

We get our information where the tunny are from the men of the trawler and drifter fleets. By that time we're already at sea in a Scarborough fishing boat - usually a thirty-five footer with a small engine - with your dinghy in tow, heading towards the drifter fleet. Once there you clamber into the dinghy, set up your rod, bait your hook with a mackerel or herring and await events.

Once you've hooked a fish you can never really say what'll happen. It took me only fifty-five minutes to bring in one tunny. On the other hand, I've played a fish for nine hours. The biggest fish I caught towed me away out of sight of the fleet. I was so intent on the game I didn't realise what was happening until it struck me that my boatman had suddenly gone a bit quiet. When I called over my shoulder, "What's the matter?" he said: "Nothing sir, but don't look round just now." Well, of course I did look round, when I found we were way out to sea without so much as a sail in sight. But all ended well, because our fishing boat came alongside just as I caught my fish - the biggest tunny I've ever caught: it weighed seven hundred and sixty-three pounds.

You can never be sure what a tunny is going to do. When it realises it's hooked it surges forward and you can feel the strain in your arms and back. The creature slackens off again and again, and each time you wonder if your thin line will hold. It's only about as thick as a matchstick. On one occasion a whale surfaced, close to the dinghy - in fact so close that I actually patted it on the back. But I've never known a hooked tunny come as close as this. When it begins to tire it may start circling the boat, and then suddenly it slackens off for the last time and you know you've won. It may be necessary to bring it up from the sea bottom and believe me this can be tiring work. You strain upwards on your rod, drop the point and reel in. Perhaps this straining up and reeling in can go on for a couple of hours, but you have an adequate reward in the first sight of your tunny. It lies in the water, an incredibly beautiful sight, anything up to nine feet of shimmering gold and green and purple and silver, a beautiful thing, shaped like a torpedo - fat in the middle and slender at the tail, with a blunt nose like that of a mackerel. When you haul it aboard the fishing boat that took you out the iridescence slowly fades. You can watch it fading, until the iridescence blends into a sort of pinky lead - that's the only way I can describe the colour - pinky lead.

The record for a tunny in the North Sea is between 850 and 900 pounds, but there's no doubt they go up to a great deal more than this. One that got away from me couldn't have been much short of half a ton. I played it for seven hours, when a friend took over the rod and played it for an hour and a half before it ultimately broke the line and got away.

In other parts of the world the tunny fisherman fishes from a power boat - perhaps a launch, but not the British tunny fisherman. But whether you use a launch in foreign waters or a dinghy at home you have a feeling of immense satisfaction when you sail for hours with a seven or eight hundred pound fish on your deck.

Times, however, were changing. While the public may still have been intrigued by the idea of such giant fish in home waters, the specialist press no longer saw tunny fishing in quite the same light. The focus of the nation's angling imagination had shifted from the vast expanses of the North Sea, to a small carp pond

Scarborough fishing vessels in 1953.

on the Welsh Border. The exploits of the Carp Catchers' Club were something any ordinary angler could relate to, far more so than the heroics of a small number of wealthy big game fishermen. In fact, even this elite group were dwindling in number. As early as 1950, a document circulated among the British Tunny Club's committee, hinting at their concerns: 'Watkinson (the Hon. Sec.) advises that the total number of subscribing members on the register at this date is 46, about half of whom were members before the war. Out of this list of pre-war members, only 8 have actively fished since the war, and of the post-war members only 11 have actively fished, the majority of these only during one season in each case.'

The 1953 and '54 seasons brought just five more tunny, on one day each season, all of them to Weatherley. The final entry in the British Tunny Club's log of certified fish was a cursory, somewhat sad note, rather than the usual elegant calligraphy. Perhaps the saddest event of all, however, was the *Fishing Gazette* obituary, in January 1954, of Richard William (Bill) Pashby. He was credited with helping land over 100 tunny, over

Testing a tunny rod in 1954!

a twenty-five year period, and his death was described as 'grievous loss' to Scarborough's fishing community. The fishermen in the harbour flew their flags at half mast, signifying not just the passing of one of their own, but unwittingly perhaps, the end of the tunny era itself.

So what had happened? Half a century later, it seems odd that one of the most incredible eras in angling history went out not with a bang, but a whimper. According to Eric Horsfall Turner, writing in the *Anglers' Annual* in 1960, a number of factors were to blame, and he was not entirely surprised by the tunny's fading popularity. 'The sudden and complete cessation,' he wrote, 'of an apparently established, or should we say re-established, sport, was not altogether unexpected to those of us who watched the way of the times.'

In many ways, he felt, the tunny season should still be a popular interlude in the annual angling calendar. 'The trout, by that time, had become indolent,' he argued, 'The Autumn salmon has never had the same appeal as the strong Spring fish

... tunny were a good fill-in for the angler, even though he could think of better types of fishing. Again, most of us are human enough to give in to the appeal of being photographed with so big a fish ... and for a man who fancies a reputation for toughness, acceptance of the North Sea game could be pleaded in evidence!'

One of the reasons, said Horsfall Turner, was the changing demographic of the population: 'Looking through the list of those who caught tunny in pre-war days, the majority were between thirty and fifty when they caught their fish. They were drawn, in the main, from the section of the population living on the upper-middle to top income scale; and in pre-war Britain thousand-a-year men could be numbered in their hundreds of thousands ... (now) only two hundred thousand men in Britain are earning £2,000 a year or more. There is no doubt that the purchasing power of £2,000 today, in terms of luxuries such as tunny fishing, is far less ... than it was for the thousands who had £1,000 a year before the war.'

Cost alone, though, was not the issue. Many anglers, he felt, could still afford the £140 or so per week that was needed to fish for tunny, but were now spending it on shark fishing instead. Horsfall Turner considered shark a vastly inferior sporting fish to the tunny, but made the point that many would-be tunny or shark hunters were not 'anglers in the fullest sense of the word'. For them, it mattered only that the quarry was sufficiently impressive, and that the fishing afforded some social opportunities, regardless of how hard the fish fought or how skilful their capture. What he termed the 'drift to shark' was less about piscatorial challenge than it was about the whims of fashion.

The situation was made worse by the fact that discerning anglers, for whom the nature of the capture was more important than the capture itself, were simply not attracted to tunny fishing any more. It had become technically, if not physically easy, the equivalent, argued Horsfall Turner, of 'being taken by

*Harry Weatherley and fish of 656lb and
579lb, caught on 22nd August, 1952.*

Weatherley and the crew of the Courage *in 1952.*

Mr Weatherley's party for crews, Scarborough, 1953:
1. E. Temple, 2. B. Crawford, 3. W. Pashby, 4. Mr Weatherley, 5. F. Watkinson, 6. G. Appleby, 7. F. Bayes,
8. M. Jenkinson, 9. T. Hunter, 10. E. Kitto, 11. J. Fletcher, 12. J. Redman, 13. T. Pashby, 14. W. Johnston,
15. W. Eves, 16. L. Price, 17. E Williams, 18. T. Crawford, 19. W. Pashby, 20. A. Ward, 21. B. Crawford,
22. C. Mainprize, 23. Councillor Whittaker.

a Japanese guide to a smooth Chuzenji basin full of big trout, shown how to bait the hook with a moth-cocoon, and allowed to pull out the fish - which has no chance of escape unless the hook hold gives way or the line breaks.'

The rigours of the North Sea meant only the most dedicated of anglers would endure it, yet the most dedicated of anglers were no longer enamoured of a sport in which success was 'merely a matter of time and physical exertion'.

This was a tough stance from an angler who had himself spent many hours seeking tunny off Scarborough, and his words ring slightly hollow when one considers that in 1956, two years after the last tunny was caught, it was the very same Eric Horsfall Turner, in the company of Tom Laughton, who was vainly chasing the few remaining herring drifters.

Whatever their reasons, nobody travelled to Scarborough in 1957 dreaming of a tunny. Some speculated that it was the fish themselves which had disappeared, but this was not entirely true. There may have been less than in the peak years of the sport, as herring numbers were also in decline, but in 1972, David Carl Forbes commented that 'The tunny are still in the North Sea, but far out from land, and the fishing is arduous, expensive and unrewarding.'

With the shortage of anglers, however, the small but dedicated band of skilled tunny skippers soon moved on and, without their expertise, any newcomers would have been hard pressed to keep the sport alive. A few old hands kept the British Tunny Club going, on paper at least, but their premises were vacated in 1960, and the financial affairs of the Club were finally wound up in 1975. Over fifty years after the first tunny were landed in Scarborough, was this, finally, the end of the line?

Nowadays, nobody speaks of tunny. The modern angler may know about tuna, even the giant bluefin variety, but the fish has long since lost its quaint English name. The 'tunny' now is not the stuff of luxury yacht-owners, glamorous rail posters and letters to *The Times*, but the preserve of museum curators, local historians and collectors of angling ephemera.

If the tunny is largely forgotten, however, the bluefin tuna is big business. Whereas the original tunny anglers struggled to sell their fish, sushi connoisseurs in Japan now pay huge prices. In 2001 a single bluefin sold for \$172,400 at Tokyo's Tsukiji Fish Market and, with such profits to be made, over-fishing has been endemic. Studies by the International Commission for the Conservation of Atlantic Tunas suggest bluefin stocks are now at just 3% of their 1960 total. Commercial long-lining still takes place, and conservationists say the bluefin tuna is effectively only one or two poor spawning years away from extinction.

And yet, despite everything, rumours still abound of a return. Tunny, to use their old name, are still seen and occasionally caught off the Irish Coast, and even Scarborough's more cynical fishermen believe a few nomads must find themselves off the Yorkshire coast from time to time. As recently as 1999, two anglers fishing off Whitby hooked fish which stripped 500 yards of line from their reels before breaking the connector knots, and tunny were thought to be the culprits.

We can only hope so. All fishermen are optimists and perhaps the time will come when, despite the ravages of long-lining and the demise of the herring fleet, some innovative angler, tired of big game fishing in warmer climes, will devise a new way of catching whatever monsters still lurk in the North Sea. Now that really would make angling history . . .

Bibliography

The following books, journals and papers were useful sources:

Anglers' Cavalcade, Eric Horsfall Turner, 1966
Big Game in British Waters, Captain W. S. Kneeshaw
Big Game Fishing in British Waters, David Carol Forbes, 1972
Modern Sea Fishing: From Bass to Tunny, Eric Cooper, 1937
Pavilions by the Sea, Tom Laughton, 1977
Sea Fishing with the Experts, Jack Thorndike, 1956
The Art of Angling, Kenneth Mansfield, 1957
The Harness of Death, W Stanley Sykes, 1932
Tunny Fishing for Beginners, Fred Taylor, 1934
Tunny Fishing L. Mitchell-Henry, 1934
BSAS Quarterly, British Sea Anglers' Society
The British Tunny Club archive
The Field
The *Fishing Gazette*
The Times

Sources of Chapter Heading Quotes

The quotes on the chapter headings were taken from
the following books:

W. Sykes, *The Harness of Death.*
L. Mitchell-Henry, *Tunny Fishing*
David Carl Forbes, *Big Game Fishing in British Waters.*
Eric Horsfall Turner, *Sea Fishing with the Experts.*
Fred Taylor, *Tunny Fishing for Beginners.*
J. A. Tansey, the *Fishing Gazette.*
Eric Cooper, *Modern Sea Fishing: From Bass to Tunny*

THE BRITISH TUNNY CLUB

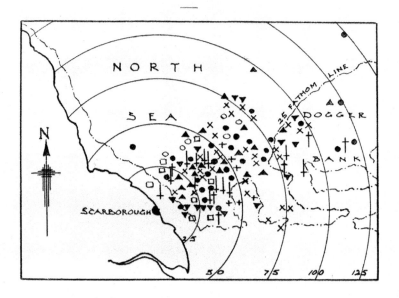

Position of tunny hooked in the North Sea.

1936	shown	by	circle
1937	,,	,,	triangle
1938	,,	,,	cross
1939	,,	,,	inverted triangle
1946	,,	,,	dagger
1947	,,	,,	inverted dagger
1948	,,	,,	circle hollow
1949	,,	,,	plus sign
1950	,,	,,	square

Markings do not necessarily mean only one fish.

Appendix B : List of Certified Fish Caught 1930-54

Fish caught and recorded in the Tunny Club annual booklet of 1951.

THE BRITISH TUNNY CLUB

LIST OF CERTIFIED FISH.

1930

	lb.	
COTTON, Lt.-Col. R. STAPLETON ...	630	B.S.A.S. Rowing Boat Certificate.
HANNAM, F. B.	591	B.S.A.S. Rowing Boat Certificate.
HARDY, H. J.	392	B.S.A.S. Rowing Boat Certificate.
MITCHELL-HENRY, L..	560	B.S.A.S. Rowing Boat Certificate.

1931

	lb.	
MITCHELL-HENRY L.	560	B.S.A.S. Rowing Boat Certificate.

1932

	lb.	
SMITH, B. CLIVE	721	B.S.A.S. Rowing Boat Certificate.
SPARROW, Col. R.	539	B.S.A.S. Rowing Boat Certificate.

1933

Green Seal denotes Certificate for Tunny of between 100 lb. and 500 lb.
Red Seal denotes Certificate for Tunny of between 500 lb. and 800 lb.
Blue Seal denotes Certificate for Tunny of between 800 lb. and over

	lb.				lb.	
BAKER, G.	763	Red Seal	ROGERS, J. E. M.		639	Red Seal
BROUGHTON, Lady	553	Red Seal	ROWLEY, Major G. S.	...	644	Red Seal
BROUGHTON, Lady	523	Red Seal	SIGRIST, F.	...	620	Red Seal
BROWN, H. A.	688	Red Seal	SOPWITH, T. O. M.	...	740	Red Seal
DUGDALE, Capt. T. L.	638	Red Seal	SOPWITH, Mrs. T. O. M.	...	505	Red Seal
FORREST, J. ...	610	Red Seal	SPRIGGS, F. S.	...	550	Red Seal
GAZE, R. P. ...	558	Red Seal	STANCLIFFE, Mrs. J.	...	630	Red Seal
LEIGH, E. ...	456	Green Seal	WILSON, A. C. ...	...	540	Red Seal
PENNY, G. ...	610	Red Seal	YULE, Miss G. M.	...	623	Red Seal
PRESTON, J. S. ...	502	Red Seal				

1934

Blue Seal denotes fish certified as caught on 100 lb. **maximum** dry b/s line.
Orange Seal denotes fish certified as caught on 130 lb. maximum dry b/s line.
Grey Seal denotes fish certified as caught on 160 lb. maximum dry b/s line.

	lb.				lb.	
BROUGHTON, Lady	738	Grey Seal	PEEL, Col. E. T.	...	641	Grey Seal
BROUGHTON, Lady	633	Grey Seal	PEEL, Col. E. T.	...	577	Grey Seal
CLARKE, R. C. R. M. ...	630	Orange Seal	PEEL, Col. E. T.	...	571	Grey Seal
CROMPTON, G. ...	663	Orange Seal	PEEL, Col. E. T.	...	539	Grey Seal
FERGUSON, R. M.	552	Orange Seal	PINNEY, G. F.	...	419	Orange Seal
GAZE, R. P. ...	489	Orange Seal	POTTER, G. W.	...	637	Orange Seal
HOLDSWORTH, J.	614	Grey Seal	ROWLEY, Major G. S.	...	489	Grey Seal
HOLGATE D. WILCOCK	764	Grey Seal	ROWLEY, Major G. S.	...	469	Grey Seal
HOLGATE, J. WILCOCK	677	Grey Seal	SHEPHERD, T. D.	...	743	Grey Seal
HOLGATE, J. WILCOCK	551	Grey Seal	SMITH, H. GIFFARD	...	798	Orange Seal
HOLGATE, M. WILCOCK	642	Grey Seal	SMITH, R. HATTERSLEY	...	679	Orange Seal
KEMPSTON, H. W.	710	Orange Seal	TAYLOR, F. ...	...	523	Orange Seal
LOVAT, Lord ...	560	Orange Seal	WEATHERLEY. H. E.	...	488	Orange Seal
PEEL, Col. E. T.	812	Grey Seal	WIGLEY, J. HAMILTON	...	589	Orange Seal
PEEL, Col. E. T.	678	Grey Seal				

1935

	lb.				lb.	
CROMPTON, G. A.	698	Grey Seal	PEEL, Col. E. T.	...	503	Grey Seal
CROMPTON, G. A.	689	Grey Seal	PEEL, Col. E. T.	...	483	Grey Seal
DENNIS, J. H.	672	Grey Seal	PEEL, Col. E. T.	...	474	Grey Seal
GALLOWAY, R. C.	521	Orange Seal	PEEL, Col. E. T.	...	449	Grey Seal
HENN, Major W. F.	542	Grey Seal	PEEL, Col. E. T.	...	444	Grey Seal
HENN, Major W. F.	484	Grey Seal	PEEL, Col. E. T.	...	435	Grey Seal

THE BRITISH TUNNY CLUB

LIST OF CERTIFIED FISH (continued).

1935

	lb.				lb.	
HODGE, The Hon. Mrs. HERMON	... 691	Grey Seal	PEEL, Col. E. T.	...	407	Grey Seal
			PEEL, Col. E. T.	...	406	Grey Seal
HOLGATE, D. WILCOCK	... 457	Orange Seal	PHILLS, P. J. V.	...	685	Orange Seal
HOLGATE, D. WILCOCK	... 635	Grey Seal	PLOWDEN, Capt. P.	...	451	Grey Seal
HOLGATE, J. WILCOCK	... 683	Orange Seal	PRIOLEAU, A. S. W.	...	720	Grey Seal
HOLGATE, J. WILCOCK	... 440	Grey Seal	ROWLEY, Major G. S.	...	606	Orange Seal
HOLGATE, M. WILCOCK	... 762	Orange Seal	SHEPHERD, T. D.	...	473	Grey Seal
HOLGATE, M. WILCOCK	... 337	Orange Seal	SHEPHERD, T. D.	...	407	Grey Seal
HOLGATE, M. WILCOCK	... 491	Grey Seal	TERRY, R.N., Lieut. A. H.		574	Orange Seal
LAMPSON, Sir MILES	... 660	Grey Seal	WHITTLE, O. LYON	...	674	Orange Seal
LAMPSON, Sir MILES	... 539	Grey Seal	WHITTLE, O. LYON	...	588	Orange Seal
O'HALLORAN, D. N. E.	... 615	Grey Seal	WILLIAMS, D. E.	...	622	Grey Seal
PEEL, Col. E. T.	... 686	Grey Seal	WILLIAMS, D. E.	...	618	Grey Seal
PEEL, Col. E. T.	... 630	Grey Seal	WROUGHTON, M. I..	...	663	Grey Seal
PEEL, Col. E. T.	... 589	Grey Seal				

1936

	lb.				lb.	
BOMFORD, H. J. P.	... 585	Grey Seal	MARRYATT, Lt.-Col. J. R.	...	540	Grey Seal
BRADSHAW, Major H. M. E.	481	Grey Seal	PEARCE, Capt. W. J.	...	539	Grey Seal
FRISBY, Capt. C. H.	658	Orange Seal	PEEL, Col. E. T.	...	573	Grey Seal
FRISBY, Capt. C. H.	618	Orange Seal	PEEL, Col. E. T.	...	547	Grey Seal
FRISBY, Capt. C. H.	394	Orange Seal	PEEL, Col. E. T.	...	457	Grey Seal
GRANT McQUEEN	661	Orange Seal	PRIOR PALMER, Major O. L.		638	Grey Seal
HOLGATE D. WILCOCK	510	Orange Seal	PRIOR PALMER, Major O. L.		595	Grey Seal
HOLGATE J. WILCOCK	614	Orange Seal	SUTCLIFFE, M.	...	479	Orange Seal
HOLGATE J. WILCOCK	516	Blue Seal	TAYLOR, F.	...	606	Grey Seal
HOLGATE M. WILCOCK	527	Orange Seal	WARD, S.	...	674	Orange Seal
HOLGATE M. WILCOCK	484	Blue Seal	PEEL, R. L. M.	...	476	Grey Seal
KEMPSTON, H. W.	434	Orange Seal	DEITER, O. B.	...	528	Grey Seal
MARRYATT, Lt.-Col. J. R.	... 604	Grey Seal	FARRINGTON, S. KIP	...	765	Blue Seal*
MARRYATT, Lt.-Col. J. R.	565	Grey Seal	FARRINGTON, S. KIP	...	753	Blue Seal*
MARRYATT, Lt.-Col. J. R.	550	Grey Seal				

* These two fish caught off Liverpool, Nova Scotia.

1937

	lb.				lb.	
BASSETT, S. G.	... 477	Orange Seal	O'HALLORAN, Capt. D. N. E.		671	Grey Seal
HAIG, N.	... 472	Grey Seal	PEEL, Col. E. T.	...	636	Grey Seal
HAYCRAFT, J. BERRY	347	Orange Seal	SUTCLIFFE, M.	...	649	Orange Seal
HENN, Major W. F.	707	Grey Seal	SUTCLIFFE, Mrs. M.	...	644	Orange Seal
JOHNSTON, R. G.	648	Orange Seal				
DOWDING, W. W.	... 581	Orange Seal	FRISBY, Capt. C. H.	...	498	Grey Seal
DOWDING, W. W.	429	Orange Seal	FRISBY, Capt. C. H.	...	584	Grey Seal
DOWDING, W. W.	511	Orange Seal	FRISBY, Capt. C. H.	...	595	Grey Seal
DOWDING, W. W.	505	Orange Seal	MATOSSIAN, J. O.	...	599	Grey Seal
FRISBY, Capt. C. H.	545	Orange Seal	MATOSSIAN, J. O.	...	611	Grey Seal
FRISBY, Capt. C. H.	658	Orange Seal	MAURICE, Lt.-Col. G.K.	...	535	Grey Seal
MAURICE, Lt.-Col. G. K.	680	Orange Seal	MAURICE, Lt.-Col. G.K.	...	479	Grey Seal
TERRY, Lieut. A. H., R.N.	670	Orange Seal	SUTCLIFFE, MARSDEN	...	492	Grey Seal
SUTCLIFFE, MARSDEN	635	Orange Seal	BAKER, Mrs. JOAN	...	383	Grey Seal

1938

	lb.				lb.	
COHEN, SAVILLE	... 643	Orange Seal	MATTHEWS, Capt. A. L.	...	481	Grey Seal
HAYCRAFT, J. BERRY	633	Orange Seal	MATTHEWS, Capt. A. L.	...	581	Grey Seal
SPARROW, Col. R.	587	Grey Seal	MATTHEWS, Capt. A. L.	...	469	Grey Seal
DOWDING, W. W.	587	Grey Seal	FIELDEN, Wing Comm. E.H.		556	Grey Seal
FRISBY, Capt. C. H.	461	Grey Seal	FIELDEN, Wing Comm. E.H.		490	Grey Seal
FRISBY, Capt. C. H.	527	Grey Seal	PEEL, Col. E. T.	...	526	Grey Seal
FRISBY, Capt. C. H.	621	Grey Seal	PEEL, J. M.	...	439	Grey Seal
FRISBY, Capt. C. H.	638	Grey Seal	HARDY, H. J.	...	532	Grey Seal
FRISBY, Capt. C. H.	623	Grey Seal	BAKER, GEORGE	...	577	Grey Seal
FRISBY, Capt. C. H.	406	Grey Seal	BARKLEY, E. T.	...	608	Grey Seal
FRISBY, Capt. C. H.	561	Grey Seal				

1939

	lb.	
HARDY, H. J.	... 667	Grey Seal

THE BRITISH TUNNY CLUB

LIST OF CERTIFIED FISH (continued).

	lb.				lb.	
			1946			
LEES, N. D.	...	530	Grey Seal	LEES, Miss M. D.	... 507	Grey Seal
LEES, N. D.	...	560	Grey Seal	WILD, MICHAEL E.	... 592	Grey Seal
FRISBY, Capt. C. H.	...	476	Orange Seal	WILD, MICHAEL E.	... 586	Grey Seal
FRISBY, Capt. C. H.	...	531	Orange Seal	WILD, MICHAEL E.	... 577	Grey Seal
FRISBY, Capt. C. H.	..	509	Orange Seal			
			1947			
WEATHERLEY, H. E.		543	Grey Seal	LAUGHTON, Major R. T. ...	536	Grey Seal
LAUGHTON, Major R. T. ...		785	Grey Seal	C.B.E.		
C.B.E.				TANSEY, J. A.	... 526	Grey Seal
LAUGHTON, Major R. T. ...		767	Grey Seal	WILD, Miss BIDI	714	Grey Seal
C.B.E.				HAMER, J. H.	... 602	Grey Seal
			1948			
TAYLOR, FRED	...	644	Grey Seal	TANSEY, J. A.	... 559	Grey Seal
TAYLOR, FRED	...	644	Grey Seal	TANSEY, J. H.	... 558	Grey Seal
TANSEY, J. A.	...	623	Grey Seal	TANSEY, J. H.	... 508	Grey Seal
			1949			
LEWIS, J. HEDLEY	...	852	Grey Seal	WEATHERLEY, H. E.	... 672	Grey Seal
COHEN, SAVILLE	...	749	Grey Seal	WEATHERLEY, H. E.	... 666	Grey Seal
COHEN, SAVILLE	...	749	Grey Seal	WEATHERLEY, H. E.	... 701	Grey Seal
TAYLOR, FRED	...	694	Grey Seal	WEATHERLEY, H. E.	... 635	Grey Seal
TAYLOR, FRED	...	740	Grey Seal	WEATHERLEY, H. E.	... 649	Grey Seal
TAYLOR, FRED	...	647	Grey Seal	WEATHERLEY, H. E.	... 613	Grey Seal
TANSEY, J. A.	...	665	Grey Seal	WEATHERLEY, H. E.	... 610	Grey Seal
TANSEY, J. A.	...	607	Grey Seal	WEATHERLEY, H. E.	... 605	Grey Seal
TANSEY, J. A.	...	596	Grey Seal	WEATHERLEY, H. E.	... 573	Grey Seal
TANSEY, J. A.	...	630	Grey Seal	WEATHERLEY, H. E.	... 487	Grey Seal
TANSEY, J. A.	...	536	Grey Seal	TURNER, E. L. H.	... 582	Grey Seal
TANSEY, J. A.	- ...	633	Grey Seal	TURNER, E. L. H.	... 467	Grey Seal
TANSEY, J. A.	...	659	Grey Seal	TURNER, E. L. H.	... 638	Grey Seal
TANSEY, J. A.	...	508	Grey Seal	PEEL, SIR E. T., K.B.E. ...	652	Grey Seal
TANSEY, J. H.	...	574	Grey Seal	PEEL, SIR E. T., K.B.E. ...	613	Grey Seal
BRADLAW, R.	...	684	Grey Seal	PEEL, SIR E. T., K.B.E. ...	536	Grey Seal
BRADLAW, R.	...	605	Grey Seal	PEEL, J. M.	... 506	Grey Seal
BRADLAW, R.	...	689	Grey Seal	PEEL, D. F.	... 701	Grey Seal
BRADLAW, R.	...	532	Grey Seal	WEATHERBY, C. N.	... 537	Grey Seal
BRADLAW, R.	...	428	Grey Seal	CROWTHER, HARRY	... 671	Grey Seal
WATKINS, A. B. K.	...	423	Blue Seal	CROWTHER, H. M.	... 534	Grey Seal
WATKINS, A. B. K.	...	696	Blue Seal	CHARRINGTON, H. N.	... 607	Grey Seal
WEATHERLEY, H. E.	...	698	Grey Seal			
			1950			
WEATHERLEY, H. E.	...	743	Grey Seal	WEATHERLEY, H. E.	... 560	Grey Seal
WEATHERLEY, H. E.	...	714	Grey Seal	WEATHERLEY, H. E.	... 545	Grey Seal
WEATHERLEY, H. E.	...	589	Grey Seal	PEEL, SIR E. T., K.B.E. ...	639	Grey Seal
WEATHERLEY, H. E.	...	561	Grey Seal			

*The following fish, caught from 1951 to 1954 are taken from the
handwritten record book of the Tunny Club.*

			1951			
WEATHERLEY, H. E.	... 617	Grey Seal	WEATHERLEY, H. E.		... 542	Grey Seal
WEATHERLEY, H. E.	... 555	Grey Seal	WASDELL, E. T.		... 642	Grey Seal
			1952			
WEATHERLEY, H. E.	... 747	Grey Seal	WEATHERLEY, H. E.		... 669	Grey Seal
WEATHERLEY, H. E.	... 742	Grey Seal	WEATHERLEY, H. E.		... 656	Grey Seal
WEATHERLEY, H. E.	... 548	Grey Seal	WEATHERLEY, H. E.		... 579	Grey Seal
WEATHERLEY, H. E.	... 640	Grey Seal				
			1953			
WEATHERLEY, H. E.	... 644	Grey Seal	WEATHERLEY, H. E.		... 538	Grey Seal
			1954			
WEATHERLEY, H. E.	... 579	Grey Seal	WEATHERLEY, H. E.		... 624	Grey Seal
WEATHERLEY, H. E.	... 660	Grey Seal				

Index